Autism and Mental Well-being in Higher Education

(2nd edition)

A practical resource for students, mentors and study skills support workers

Dr Susy Ridout

Illustrations by:
Catherine Haywood
James Mycock

Pavilion

Autism and Mental Well-being in Higher Education (2nd edition)

A practical resource for students, mentors and study skills support workers

Published by:
Pavilion Publishing and Media Ltd
Blue Sky Offices
Cecil Pashley Way
Shoreham by Sea
West Sussex
BN43 5FF
UK

Tel: 01273 43 49 43
Email: info@pavpub.com
Web: www.pavpub.com

First published 2020

A catalogue record for this book is available from the British Library.

ISBN: 978-1-913414-01-6

Pavilion is the leading publisher and provider of professional development products and services for workers in the health, social care, education and community safety sectors. We believe that everyone has the right to fulfill their potential and we strive to supply products and services that help raise standards, promote best practices and support continuing professional development.

Author: Susy Ridout
Cover design: James Mycock
Illustrations: Catherine Haywood and James Mycock
Editor: Ruth Chalmers, Pavilion Publishing and Media Ltd
Page layout and typesetting: Emma Dawe, Pavilion Publishing and Media Ltd
Printing: CMP Digital Print Solutions

Testimonials

'What a fantastic resource this is for those interested in how to support autistic students and for autistic students wanting excellent information around how to navigate university. Susy's writing may very well prove, for some, to make the difference between succeeding at university and not. A superb book which should be read by anyone at university involved with autistic students, and stocked by all universities so it's available for their autistic students.'

Dr Luke Beardon, Senior Lecturer in Autism, Sheffield Hallam University

'Susy Ridout has done an excellent job of writing in an engaging and reassuring way a guide that demystifies the mentoring process and will enable students and mentors to get the most out of their time together. This is an excellent book – I'd recommend it to students of all ages. It is a well put together and clearly written resource that will have you going back to it time and time again as you continue on your HE journey.

The book is a comprehensive guide that covers not only the academic side of Higher Education but also friendships and more practical day to day skills that can often be forgotten in the upheaval of starting in Higher Education.'

Kabie Brook, Chair of Autism Rights Group Highland

'I have had experience of university as an undiagnosed adult in the 1970s and as a diagnosed adult who returned to education more recently. Having experienced difficulties in both environments, I found mentoring to be very useful in helping me recover from my initial bad experiences and as such I can fully endorse Susy's book.

There is no doubt when I first went to university after high school, that I found both the social and academic environment to be thoroughly perplexing after the regimentation of my former school. I do not think anything has changed a great deal since so far as the challenges to an autistic student go. I had difficulties coping with the differences in learning styles and the reliance on self-organisation as well as integrating within a different social environment, with the challenges of freshers' week, making friends and trying to fit in. I did not cope well with independent study and ultimately fell behind with my finals because nobody had realised the problems I had in coping with university life.

My second chance came as a mature student. To begin with, I did not find it a lot easier and got into difficulties for a different set of reasons. However, a second assessment for disabled students' allowance provided me with funds for a mentor. My experiences improved after that and I can fully appreciate in retrospect what was lacking in my former experience.

Susy has set forth a very plain and autistic-friendly exposition of what can be gained from the mentoring experience and provides a very practical guide that I wish had been available when I was starting out. Susy fully understands the perspectives of people like myself who find themselves very much in the deep end of social and academic experience through no fault of our own. This is a useful book both for students who are unsure as to what mentoring involves, and for those who are considering taking up the role of mentoring.'

Dr Larry Arnold, Editor and public speaker

'Getting the most out of university life and study can be a challenge for many students. It is also a challenge for universities in terms of providing accessibility and flexibility that takes account of diversity within the student group. Based on her years of insider experience supporting autistic students, Susy Ridout provides a handbook that is equally useful for students and those providing mentorship or support. It combines the everyday and the practical with a sophisticated theoretical underpinning that recognises the inter-related issues of neurodiversity and intersectionality. This challenges the more traditional disability paradigm in which autism (and by implication) autistic people are seen as a problem, and solutions are seen in terms of autistic people having to accommodate to and fit in with social, sensory and learning environments which are profoundly unsuitable and oppressive.'

Professor Jerry Tew, Mental Health and Social Work, Director of Family Potential Research Centre and Head of Education, School of Social Policy at the University of Birmingham

'For all young people, going to university is a challenge representing novel demands and the need for rapid adjustment. It represents a change of lifestyle that involves new surroundings, new friends, different customs, new living arrangements and the demands of a new academic environment. This can be exciting and fun but many may also be overwhelming. For autistic students this challenge can be even more daunting. This clearly written, straightforward guide draws extensively on the autistic experience and research and practice to approach this challenge. Susy Ridout is to be commended in producing this guide, which is packed full of resources, good advice and sensible suggestions. It will become an indispensable resource for all involved with the support of young people at university, especially those students who may struggle with making new social relationships, the novelty of change or are autistic.'

Richard Mills, Research Director Research Autism, Research Fellow, CAAR, University of Bath

This book is dedicated to my sons Patrick and Isidro.
You are a constant source of energy and have made me so proud.
Keep reaching for your dreams.

Contents

Acknowledgements

I owe so much to the many students and other individuals that I have worked with over the years in either a mentoring or academic support capacity. You are amazingly talented, fun and interesting people, and without the time that we have spent together exploring and addressing the barriers to learning, and what constitutes an enabling environment, this book would not have materialised. The comments of some students that have been included give an edge to this book by illustrating so well the points being made, and I thank those of you who engaged with this aspect. Dr Damian Milton (Lecturer in Intellectual and Developmental Disabilities, Tizard Centre, University of Kent), Kabie Brook (Chair, Autistic Rights Group Highland, ARGH) and Sarah Richards, thank you for your devoted time spent reading through the draft and providing critical and sensitive comments. Thank you also Barbara Walker for your timely advice about working with illustrators, and particular thanks go to James Mycock and Catherine Haywood, who have brought the book to life with their illustrations. Finally, but not least, thanks go to the publishers who have supported me, and particularly my editor, Ruth Chalmers, who has guided me through this process.

Important in this list are all those individuals, too many to mention, who have supported me in a range of aspects relating to my own life journey throughout the writing of this book – you know who you are.

Responsibility for the final text including terminology, references and mistakes is mine alone.

About the illustrators

Catherine Haywood is an ex-student with a hoard of plastic toys, an addiction to chocolate, and an incredible level of sympathy for small things. She is also in possession of a BTEC in Fine Art and a BA in Animation with Honours, as well as a deep concern for when she makes a list longer or shorter than three items in a single sentence.

James Mycock is an illustrator and printmaker based in Birmingham. James is in his third year of university, studying Illustration and has been mentored by Susy for the past two years. He fervently believes in the importance of mentoring, not just for its academic benefits but also in its ability to nurture self-confidence and self-development. Outside of the visual arts, James' interests include classical music, literature and Belgian comics.

About the author

Dr Susy Ridout, Mentor, Academic Support Worker, Author and Researcher (autism, disability and sexual violence)

Susy has worked as a mentor and academic skills support worker with autistic and disabled people in higher education for a decade. Seeing mentoring as an opportunity to explore issues relating to both disclosure and well-being within a number of settings, including higher education and employment scenarios, Susy was also a mentor for the Cygnet Mentoring Project (a research pilot designed and delivered by autistic/neurodivergent individuals for autistic individuals). Having also benefited from mentoring, she uses it as an approach to examine barriers to learning, develop effective coping strategies, investigate what constitutes enabling learning environments and explore terminology used to voice these. Completion of her doctorate (University of Birmingham, 2016), highlighted the use of mixed media as a means to locate the autistic voice to the fore in research, services and debate. Susy has taken this forward to extend her research as a member of PARC (the Participatory Autism Research Collective), where she is an Independent Researcher. Susy continues to mentor throughout the UK and apply her research to a range of issues including neurodivergence and sexual violence.

Foreword

Dr Damian Milton, Tizard Centre, University of Kent

Recent years have seen an ever growing body of evidence to support mentoring as a potentially useful way of helping autistic people to reach their goals, particularly when delivered in a person-centered way and sensitive to autistic experiences. Every year the numbers of autistic people entering post-compulsory education and seeking support for their needs is increasing. In this inclusive and accessible book, Susy Ridout demonstrates her many years of experience of working as a mentor with autistic people in varying contexts, and clearly exemplifies an ethos of centering such work on what she has learnt from those for whom mentoring has the most impact; the mentees themselves.

The content in this book covers a plethora of advice relating to fundamental issues to consider in mentoring practice with autistic people, from the boundaries of the mentor and mentee roles and goal setting, to building academic skills. The book also contains very welcome information regarding how to cope with the anxiety of being assigned a mentor and not knowing what to expect, liaising with tutors, living with other students, money management, managing stress, disclosure and intersectionality (to name but some of the issues explored).

The information and guidance contained in this book is also matched with helpful activities for mentors and mentees to share, explore together, adapt and add to. Throughout this book a reflective, flexible and sensitive approach is taken to the issues at hand. A variety of approaches are offered and some advice may be more salient than others to the reader, but this will differ for each individual.

The new chapters that have been added to this second edition skillfully add depth on much needed subjects that impact on the lives of autistic students such as sexual violence. The importance of intersectionality and wider social and cultural influences are expanded upon and I fully endorse the participatory and progressive ethos embodied in the creative process of updating this most useful guide.

I have personally known Susy for many years, having been colleagues as doctoral researchers at the University of Birmingham, as well as in a number of projects, such as the Theorising Autism Project (TAP), The Participatory Autism Research Collective (PARC), and the Research Autism/Cygnet Mentoring Project, and it is a joy to see this book being written and becoming available to a wider audience.

I hope this book will be widely read, particularly by those working in disability support services in higher (and indeed further) education establishments, but also students, student union officers, disability and well-being teams, and all those providing lecturing, tutoring and pastoral support to students. Most importantly, this book will be of great use to autistic students navigating the higher education environment and acquiring the support that they require and have every right to.

Beautifully illustrated by Catherine Haywood and James Mycock, as far as I'm aware this book is the first of its kind to specifically explore mentoring practice in relation to autistic people, and differs from previous available guidance by being rooted in the social model of disability and neurodiversity paradigm. It sits alongside the work of Susy's colleagues within the Participatory Autism Research Collective (PARC) as a force for challenging current practices and improving upon them. The book provides a most helpful reference for both mentor and mentee to keep on track and meet their agreed targets and help stimulate discussion and potential support needs with one another respectfully. The strategies and guidance contained in this book can aid autistic people to achieve greater autonomy in their lives, and I thoroughly recommend it.

Introduction

Reason for this book

This book follows nine years where I have mentored and provided academic support to autistic and disabled students in higher education (HE) and also employment. The origins of the book lie in the reality that, whilst support is being offered to students through Disability Support Allowance (DSA), most students have little idea as to what mentoring entails or that in its ideal form it should cater for the needs of the individual. In other words, it should be person-centered.

On meeting me for the first time, many students express anxiety about not understanding what mentoring or academic support is, so this year I decided to draw together some of the key areas that have been raised by students. I have addressed these by adding some activities that could help both students and mentors/academic support workers engage with each other in the early stages and beyond. These have been addressed in different sections.

Assembling your tool box

In each section, I have provided a couple of activities. I would encourage students and mentors to add to these, or adapt them according to requirements, and my past experience has highlighted the benefit of reflecting on what does or does not work for you as an individual. Keep a record of this and build on activities as this is your tool box of strategies that you can take with you on your journey through HE and into the employment sector.

Valuing yourself

This book is ultimately about gradually learning to do this for yourself so that you have more control over your life, your expressed identities, the ability to transfer your skills and knowledge and, most importantly, to see yourself as the valuable member of the community that you are, with great choices for your future.

Sometimes the activities have been a student's idea, sometimes my own or something that we have discovered together. It is perhaps clear that individual students will have a mixture of good and bad past experiences that they bring to sessions, such is life, and in order to move forwards it is often necessary to reflect back. This is a strength which can add fresh insight with very real benefits. Use the book to explore those areas that are relevant to you.

Updates to this edition

Following the success of the first edition of this book, which reflected the many voices of autistic students with whom I have worked, it was apparent that new chapters needed to be added to better reflect diversity and to acknowledge the prevalence of sexual violence on campus. With this in mind, Chapter 13 is on gender and explores such issues as identity, disclosure, pronouns, name change and transitioning. The second new chapter, Chapter 14, addresses issues experienced by many individuals from BAME communities, such as acceptance within their own culture, language barriers, obtaining a diagnosis, tokenism and inclusion of BAME voices within HE. The third additional chapter (15) addresses sexual violence, whether it has happened prior to university or during studies and on or off campus. This chapter discusses processing and communicating what has happened and support options avilable.

Final word

Each and every single student that I work with has brought new insight into the fascinating field of autism, disability and neurodivergence and has emphasised the fact that working together can facilitate the building of successful approaches to tackling barriers to learning. I would like to thank you all for this amazing experience and hope that you enjoy this book as much as I have enjoyed writing it.

Resources

The resources in the Appendices are available to download and print from: www.pavpub.com/autism-mental-wellbeing-in-higher-education-resources

Part 1:
University life and support for autistic students and students with mental health needs

Chapter 1: Mentoring support

Role boundaries of the mentor

Having been provided with a mentor, it is important to know what their role is and the boundaries within which they will work. Firstly, they are contracted by the university to provide mentoring support to you, and this is very different from coaching, buddying or friendship roles.

Among their duties a mentor is there to offer a professional perspective. They are there to:

- Listen to your concerns.
- Assist you in developing strategies to cope with difficult situations.
- Help liaise with tutors.
- Update your disability support worker with any changes in your circumstances.
- Liaise with other team members as required.
- Consider perspectives on situations and help you think these through together with possible outcomes.
- Pay attention to safeguarding.
- Offer a combination of support, challenges and constructive criticism to enable you to reach your goals and the way which best suits your learning style.
- Facilitate discussion of both long-term and short-term goals.
- Support you in managing your whole student experiences, academic, social and in relation to your well-being.
- Liaise with you and the university academic support team if needed.

Mentoring and what to expect

If you have been provided with a mentor, they will be able to explain to you the purpose of mentoring and how you can make the most of it. You can prepare yourself for the first session in case you are anxious:

**Bring something that interests you
(some of your work) to show or talk about.**

Your mentor will be able to find out about your interests and skills by looking at your work and together you can find ways to talk about it.

You may also have questions you want to ask about your mentor. After all, they are someone who will be supporting you, so it is important that they can work in a way that is sensitive to your needs. Here is what one student felt about their mentoring:

> 'I have always thought I have got someone to talk to when I have mentoring whenever I get anxious and stressed.'

Setting goals

A key part of mentoring is setting some goals you want to work towards. You may know what you would like to explore, or you may need to talk this through/think about this visually with your mentor. It is best to set 3-4 goals, and these can be changed as they are achieved or if you need to prioritise others.

Goals may fall into a number of areas such as:

- Becoming more organised (this may be in relation to university work).
- Building a social network.
- Developing independent living skills.
- Well-being (tackling issues that impact negatively on you).
- Looking at how your current course fits into your overall career/life plan.

Other areas may be identified with your mentor.

Review of goals

Looking at the type of support that you would like is fundamental in helping you to make progress. Developing a plan of work and targets is a crucial part of this, and as a visual display can encourage you. So establishing goals is an excellent way of organising your work and progress, and this can be reviewed regularly.

As individuals, we all have good and bad moments, and it is in the latter moments that we may feel that there is no progress made or that all progress has been lost. By having a plan, your mentor can help you review this and keep you on target (Research Autism, 2015; Ridout and Edmondson, 2017).

Skills audit

Doing a skills audit can be a really useful thing to do in the early stages of your course, and provides a good way for you and your mentor to get to know each other. Map out or list the following:

- Reason(s) for choosing this course.

- Skills that you bring to this course.

- Skills that you would like to develop, if possible.

You may not be sure of the answer(s) to all of these, but you can use it as a piece of work in progress that you add to or adapt from time-to-time.

Breaking down tasks

Tasks can often seem overwhelming, leaving you with a sense of not knowing where or how to start. The problem with this is that if left unaddressed, this can result in a number of tasks building up and you feeling increasingly under pressure.

> **Tip: Manage tasks by 'chunking', or breaking them down into more manageable pieces.**
> **It helps because:**
> - **you can see your progress better**
> - **you can reflect on your progress**
> - **you do not become overwhelmed.**

Students tackle this activity in a variety of ways according to the course that they are on.

> **Example of chunking used by an illustration student, who had to produce images for an assignment:**
> - **Setting themselves the goal of doing an hour of work each evening, which might cover:**
>   - **rough sketches**
>   - **producing 1 main image**
>   - **exploring a new medium.**

Pacing mentoring or study sessions

Sessions should be established with the individual in mind as the support requirements of each are distinct. As good practice, I would advocate looking at an agenda using one of two approaches. This has worked with individual students and me over the past ten years:

1. More informal and set according to issues arising, and although this addresses goals, it is more flexible and can respond to rapid change; sessions should occur as often as required, but also take into consideration allocated hours.

2. Formal with longer term goals set. You could mark these on a 'Salmon Line' by using a scale of 0-10 to indicate how you progress each week, where 0 would show no progress in respect of the goal chosen and 10 would indicate that you had achieved your goal (Research Autism, 2015; Ridout and Edmondson, 2017). Again, sessions should occur as often as required, but also take into consideration allocated hours.

Familiarise yourself with the university environment

For many autistic students in particular, change and the transition to new environments can be daunting, so asking a familiar person or your mentor to help you explore the university campus and facilities will help you settle in. This is also important to help reduce anxieties when new subjects or modules are introduced. Things you may wish to look at include:

- summer school (some disability support teams run these)
- attending fresher's week with a familiar person
- lecture theatres
- seminar rooms
- workshops
- locating tutor rooms
- finding the library and checking its layout
- checking out eating areas
- sourcing quiet areas
- finding student services
- locating the students' union
- accommodation office.

You may want to discuss with your mentor any strategies you use to help you access these areas, so that if there are any changes, they can help you work with your strategy toolkit.

Last-minute changes of timetabled rooms

Tutors can help if they are aware of room changes as there may be a demand for certain rooms.

You or your mentor can re-emphasise any difficulties you experience with change (and if you have a support statement, this should be written into it).

> **You could ask your mentor to support you in asking for an email/text from your tutor regarding any changes in advance – this helps with processing of new information and helps you to build coping strategies and avoid becoming over-anxious.**

Visiting new areas

If it is difficult for you to visit new areas, try to discuss this with your mentor. You may be able to go together to a new venue e.g. a new café area on campus, or a new social group.

Gentle encouragement to try new, preference-related activities is good. It helps you to develop your confidence, build on your self-esteem and enables you to develop your independence.

Venues to visit (course-related)

Many of the courses at your university will have visits to other venues or places around the locality built in to course activities. It may be a good idea to visit the university area on a weekend or evening prior to the start of term to see what it has to offer. This can help you feel more relaxed when you start your course. There are many maps to help you discover what an area has to offer, and this may entail a good weekend or evening activity either prior to starting university or in the early part of your course.

Areas of interest

You may have arrived at university with interests that you love doing and some that you would like to pursue further, perhaps with a group of friends. As stated in the section about friendships (Chapter 4), there are many already-established groups for you to join at the university. If there isn't one in your area of interest, you may wish to set one up, and if you need support to do this, your mentor or the students' union can help with this.

Activity 1.1: Reviewing your interests

In addition to the interests that you already have, consider those that you might like to explore.

- If you have moved to a new town to study, there might be a number of different opportunities both in and outside the university.

- If you are still in the same town, simply studying at a different level provides you with a range of new opportunities and facilities to broaden your skills and knowledge area.

Remember ... developing interests and skills is an excellent resource as these can be added to your CV.

Activity 1.2: Draw a mind map and add to this

On a large piece of paper, map out your interests. Consider the following:

- How long have you been doing these?
- Why do you enjoy each of these?
- How do you want to develop them?
- Do they link in with or compliment your course?
- What skills/knowledge do each of these activities develop?
- Are these activities/interests you like to do alone, or with others?
- Would you like to access similar groups at university?
- Do you need support to do this?

This activity is invaluable for assessing your skills and knowledge. This is an area that employers often like to talk about.

Activity 1.3: Exploring new activities in your area

Whether you are in a new town or your home town, familiarising yourself with new activities that may compliment your course or develop new skills is a good idea. In addition, it can help you settle into a new environment.

In your mentoring sessions, or on your own, you could explore events, museums, galleries, local writers' groups, competitions, cafés where information is put or a range of different, quiet areas for you to work.

You may like to do this activity and take photos of a place you like so that you can discuss these with your mentor and look at how you can become involved in events. An example of this may include a local theatre that puts on a range of small to larger scale touring events and activities. Better still, there might be local festival events, so think about getting involved!

There might be different opportunities to develop new or existing skills and make new friends and contacts. In addition, these are great opportunities for networking.

Becoming independent and setting your own agenda

Think about control and choice you would like in your life.

You and your mentor may look at you gradually setting the agenda for these sessions, if you are not already doing so. You may have a good idea of the following issues, and these will all be relevant to these sessions:

- Your well-being.
- How you are managing the course.
- Friendships.
- Accommodation.

Do you like the type of accommodation where you are living this year?

You may want a change of living circumstances in the second year, and this choice is all part of student life. Discuss options with family, friends and your mentor and see what is best for you.

The students' union/university website may produce a handy information sheet about what to look for in accommodation (either privately owned or let by the university), and of course you may choose to live at home.

Tips for mentors and study skills support workers

- Understand the difference between mentoring, coaching, buddying, friendship and study skills support roles, as there are clear differences which you and students you are working with should understand.

- Plan the first session to include some introductory activities in case the student finds talking to new people challenging.

- Familiarise yourself with the student's course.

- Bring something to talk about e.g. about the university and the course being studied.

- Check whether the student would like you to have a copy of their support statement, as it is sent to their head of course to inform tutors (not all universities do this as a matter of course).

- Check the availability of quiet areas.

- Check how individual students like to do things e.g. setting tasks to do between sessions or setting an agenda at the beginning or end of a session.

- Discuss the student's communication preferences with them e.g. text, email.

■ Discuss what areas of the university to visit with the student in terms of their course and relaxation. This is an excellent way of helping students settle into a new environment.

■ Help your student(s) by discussing activities they would like to develop both in and outside university; also discuss the advantages of each, for example skills to put on their CV, or developing friends and social networks.

■ Look at a map with your student(s) to familiarise yourself with a list of local activity venues such as cinemas, theatres, Comic-Con events, pubs with music, galleries, museums and sports venues, and support them in planning some relaxation time.

Chapter 2:
Academic support

University support

Universities provide academic support through staff on campus, so your mentoring and academic support will now be separate.

Each university will have plenty of support for students, and this chapter details how you can:

- obtain your tutor's help
- build coping strategies
- manage your workload
- address time management
- tackle assignments
- identify available resources.

Overview of the course

Familiarising yourself with the aspects of the course that will be taught on a term-by-term basis is key to helping you settle into university life. Knowing when you will be doing course work and when this will feed into assignments, presentations or practical work is vital.

The modules you choose for your course will not necessarily be the same as others. Whilst tutors will have planned for these, individual students have different requirements, and if it is helpful for you to have a copy of handouts or lecture notes (in a hard copy or on the Learning Management System (LMS) website) in advance, it can be useful for tutors to understand the reason behind this. This should be explained in your support statement which is sent to the head of department by your disability support worker.

> **Module options can help you:**
> - **develop skills in new areas**
> - **build on existing skills.**

Tutors

Every student has a **personal tutor**, and this will probably change each year. In addition, you will also have a **module tutor** for each module studied. Sometimes they might be the same person. It is important that you know who your tutors are as they are there to help you.

Your mentor can help you identify the tutor if you are unsure.

You may also wish to have a meeting early on or regularly throughout the course to help you deal with anxieties and ensure you are keeping up-to-date with everything.

Working with tutors helps build their knowledge and expertise on the diversity of students, whilst seeing you as individuals with specific support requirements which may or may not be similar to others.

Liaising with tutors

If you are confident to liaise with your tutor when you need to, that is great. However, some of you may wish to ask your mentor to support you and to attend a tutorial with you. If you would like, they can also help you to ask questions and take notes. You can also ask members of the academic support team to help you as well.

Some examples where you may require additional tutor support are:

- **To clarify an assignment with a mentor present.**
- **To break down the management of an assignment with regular tutorials in between.**
- **To manage anxiety around presentations and discuss options.**

Feedback

Your tutor will give you feedback individually about your assignments and coursework unless it is a group presentation. However, as a disabled student, your support statement will state that you might benefit from regular, individual tutorials, and this can also include feedback sessions. Your mentor can attend a session with your tutor with you and help you to understand the feedback.

Time to process information

It may be useful for you to ask tutors to send an email with information about a lecture/module/tutorial prior to meetings, setting out the goals and any relevant dates.

Similarly, emails after meetings to confirm information discussed and decisions made may also assist you in reviewing learning points either individually or with your academic skills support worker.

Reviewing progress

Tutors are there to help you, so if you would like feedback on your progress and to talk about how you can improve your work in any way, ask.

You can:

- email them
- have a meeting with your mentor
- have a meeting with your disability support worker, mentor and tutor and develop an action plan.

Reviews can be particularly helpful if you are finding certain aspects of the course difficult. This way, support can be adjusted to suit your requirements.

Talking to people early on about any problems can help avoid stress.

Reflection on work and progress (reacting to criticism)

Receiving criticism about your work is often difficult. However, it is a fact that, as individuals, we learn most from our mistakes. The feedback given by your tutors/lecturers is designed to help you improve your work against targets set for each module.

As you prepare your work, think about where your work might fit within these targets. Your mentor and study skills support worker(s) will help you to do this.

Ask yourself:

- Am I answering the question?
- Am I giving relevant references?
- Have I thought about my work structure and addressed this?

Assignments

Planning assignments

1. Analyse the question. What type of assignment is it?

    - An **account** of something:
        - Describe and explore.
        - Less emphasis on giving opinions.
    - An **argument** where there are two (or more) sides.
    - A **comparison weighs up**:
        - problems
        - benefits.

2. Think about an answer.

    - Make lists.
    - Draw mind maps (where you plot and link ideas on paper i.e. you have a main theme with many related ideas and then each have their own related sub-themes). This builds a picture of what you may wish to talk about.
    - Look at the assignment from different perspectives by using these 'Wh/H' questions: who, what, when, where, why, how. To help you remember, this is called **cubing** as a cube has six sides and there are six main types of question.

    This will help you look at **who** you are addressing (for example); **what** you want your reader to know; **when** the event took place i.e. the timeline; **where** exactly you are talking about (country, region, establishment etc); **why** the study topic is important; **how** it impacts on your research/study field.

3. Plan the answer.

    - Introduction.
    - Body of text including:
        - headings
        - paragraphs
        - conclusion.

4. Write the answer.

    - The topic sentence of the introduction states the main idea of the paragraph, and introduces the themes of the essay. (The topic sentence is generally the first sentence, and it introduces the paragraph. The final sentence of a paragraph should lead into the next.)

- The final sentence of the introduction leads into the main body of the assignment.
- If you are **developing an argument**, you should support each statement with logical rationale. You should use references to provide evidence to support your argument, and this makes your argument more convincing.
- If you are **arguing** a case, give a balanced account with alternative viewpoints and use references.
- The **conclusion** usually begins with a concluding phrase such as:
  - in general
  - to sum up
  - in conclusion
  - to conclude.

5. Check the answer:
   - Have you completed the task?
   - Have you answered all parts of the question?
   - Check the:
     - grammar
     - spelling
     - punctuation
     - word count
     - references
     - font (size, type and spacing).
   - Have you added your name?

Written assignments

It is important that as soon as you are given an assignment that you start to reflect on it and how it fits into the module you are being/have been taught. Leaving the assignment to the last minute will not allow you to develop good planning skills (an essential part of your academic development), explore ways that you can liaise with your tutor and obtain feedback, or assist you in the management of any anxiety. For this reason, as soon as you have an assignment it is useful to get into the habit of developing the following practice, bearing in mind that each assignment will develop at a different pace:

- Open a Word document.
- Put a heading at the top of the page (this can be changed later if necessary) and call this **Heading 1** by going to the settings at the top of the page.

- Put in main sub-headings using **Heading 2** e.g:
    - Introduction.
    - Other sub-headings according to key areas you wish to cover.
    - Conclusion.
    - References.
    - Bibliography.
- Add bullet points of key areas to address under each sub-heading.
- Develop bullet points into sentences, then phrases, then work related phrases into a paragraph.

Note that for some assignments, tutors will ask you to merge the references and bibliography.

Group work

Group work is a part of most courses at some point, and it is fair to say that in the many years that I have mentored the same challenges keep arising. However, these could be avoided with good planning and an understanding of individual students. Common issues are:

- Not being helped to join a group in the first place.
  Solution: ask your tutor or mentor to support you as your support statement should state that you require this.

- Tutors may not know you have a support summary.
  Solution: either you, your mentor, or disability support worker can let them know so they can read this and ask questions if needed.

- Group cliques can leave you feeling left out.
  Solution: ask your tutor or mentor for help.

- Difficulty filtering and reading body language may make it harder to understand the intentions of other group members.
  Solution: talk to your mentor and tutor about what works for you. If you are unsure, explore this with your mentor. Self-awareness is your best strategy.

- You prefer to work alone as it is difficult discussing and listening to the ideas of other group members.
  Solution: ask your mentor/support worker to join you in these sessions. Working with others is a good skill to build up, so ask your tutor/mentor/support worker for help.

- Difficulty communicating ideas to the group.
  Solution: talk to your mentor about different ways to tackle this. Perhaps better group task planning will enable you to write down/mind map some thoughts for each session in advance.

- Others in the group do not turn up to plan or do their work and the work is marked as a whole group piece.
  Solution:

  1. Email the others and explain the problem telling them that this is worrying you.

  2. Ask your tutor or mentor for help.

- You don't get on with others in the group
  Solution:

  1. Ask your tutor if you can switch groups.

  2. Sometimes we need to be able to get on with others who are different, so try to remain focused on the task.

Presentations

If you have a support statement, you will be allowed to negotiate a number of aspects of the presentation such as:

- the setting, so that it has a lower level of sensory stimuli

- the order in which you present, especially if this helps you lower your anxiety

- possibly even the format.

Of course this is more difficult to resolve if it is a group presentation, but if your tutor is sensitive to your support requirements, then you will be working in a group that enables you to work to your best ability.

Reflection on work and progress (providing criticism)

As part of your course, you may be asked to provide feedback to each other. It may help you to think of ways in which you find criticism helpful. For example:

- Do you find it easier if someone comments on the things that have worked well first before commenting on the areas that you could improve?

- Is it easier if you look at how well someone has addressed the question and go through this?

- Are you able to make a comparison with some earlier work of theirs and talk about areas that have improved or which require attention?

Time management

Managing assignment deadlines

During your course you will be given a number of assignments with deadlines that may be very close together. Managing your assignments well and structuring them so that you can progress several at a time, switching attention between them when you feel stuck or need a break, are all ways of effectively managing time and stress.

There are several ways to manage your time:
- **Diary.**
- **Sticky notes on a computer.**
- **Post-it notes on a notice board.**
- **Using the alarm on your mobile.**
- **Using a daily/weekly planner.**

Daily planner (see Appendix 1)

A must-have for students is a diary, whether this is on your phone or a hard copy.

- Update this daily.
- Look at it each evening so that you can prepare for the next day.
- Establish a routine with this activity to help you stay up-to-date with work. You can also add relaxation time, and this allows you to manage your anxiety in a number of ways. For example:
  - Identifying problems early, so strategies can be worked out with your tutors, mentor or disability support worker.
  - Seeing patterns and acting on them enables you to find a solution/help yourself. This may be to do with a particular module you find tricky, and which you could do with having explained differently.
  - Timetables will change throughout the course, so you can keep a check on this.

Weekly planner (see Appendix 2)

In addition to the daily planner, you need to know what you are going to be doing on a weekly basis. Keep a record of:

- lectures/timetable
- assignments and deadlines
- presentations and deadlines
- other coursework and deadlines
- tutorials
- seminars
- mentoring/academic support sessions
- well-being appointments
- fun activities.

Again you can do this using your phone, or a hard copy. You may wish to print off a copy to keep on your notice board too.

Maintaining folders

Set up a folder for each module with dividers to separate each week. This will allow you to place notes in the correct section and helps if you miss sessions or are revising.

> **Organising yourself from the outset will help you manage both work and anxiety.**

Identify deadlines

- Use a template/worksheet to record targets and deadlines set in discussions.
- Check the deadline – your project brief will state this and your mentor or tutor can help you.
- Make sure that any extra time you are allowed for your disability is added (check this with your mentor or your disability support worker).
- Plan a timeline for your work. This is very important as you may have more than one assignment at once and this entails you working on sections gradually to progress your work e.g. the introduction, one key sub-section at a time, the conclusion, checking the references and finally write the abstract.

Your tutor can check that you understand the brief, the deadline and the process for handing the work in.

This can be done using your preferred form of communication, but is also best confirmed by email.

Meeting targets/deadlines

If you have a support statement because of a disability, this will include any extensions you have for assignments as follows:

Assignment less than 1,500 words = **5 extra working days**.

Assignment 1,500 to 4,000 words = **7 extra working days**.

Assignment 4,000 words and above = **10 extra working days**.

Check with your disability support worker that you are working to the right deadline, especially if the deadline occurs over a holiday/bank holiday.

Resources

Setting up your university email account

As a student, you will be given an email account which you need to set up with your password. Although you may have given another email to your mentor and the disability team, your tutors and other staff across the university will use your university account. You should check your university account daily.

Using the university Learning Management System

These are the most typically used online Learning Management Systems (LMS) across universities. For example, two of the most commonly used are Moodle or Canvas. It is important to familiarise yourself with these as they contain details of:

- lecture slides
- assignments
- deadlines

■ exam dates

■ other information necessary for your course.

Some students find this easy to navigate, whilst others do not. Either way you are not alone! There is plenty of support within your department and IT help on campus. You can also ask your mentor and academic skills support worker for help.

The library

The library will have collated and organised a lot of very useful information, and there will be several staff members to help you.

■ There may be a named library specialist in your subject, who can show you around the relevant book and journal sections both in hard copy and on the library catalogue.

■ Look for specialist leaflets identifying the relevant library sections for each subject.

■ For disabled students, there might be a room that can be booked at the library desk or online for quiet study.

■ There may also be other rooms for quiet study, which can also be booked.

Referencing

The library will have lots of information about the referencing system your university/department wishes you to use. You should become familiar with this as early as possible. Your mentor and study skills support worker(s) can help you.

Each assignment requires you to use this referencing format, so the sooner you familiarise yourself with this the better. Again your mentor or advisors in the university academic/study centre will be able to support you with this.

Endnote

Endnote is a referencing system which allows you to enter the information about each reference you select. You can use this with your assignments to insert references in the style required by your university (set by you). These will then appear both within the text (in date order at the point chosen) and in the references section in alphabetical order. This is invaluable for all students, but particularly people who find scrolling up and down large amounts of text very tiring. It is also excellent for those with dyslexia, Irlen Syndrome and epilepsy, in addition to many other students.

OneNote

OneNote may have come with software allocated to your through your DSA and is an excellent way of keeping your notes and files organised.

For example, you can do this for each module and assignment and copy and paste relevant notes and images as required.

LinkedIn account (also see Chapter 19 on employment)

For some courses, developing a LinkedIn account is a course assignment. However, you may also find it useful to have one for linking with professionals, practitioners and employers in your field. Your mentor and study skill support worker may be able to work with you to set an account up or signpost you to others who can do this with you.

Think of some positive things that you can put into your profile and regularly build on this adding to the fields as relevant.

Maintaining a blog

As courses change, so do ways of recording work, and some of you may already be familiar with blogs or even have one or more that are active. However, setting up a blog is something that you may be asked to do as part of your course work, and you will be given support and guidance to do this. This can tap into your creative flair or encourage you to express your views on a range of matters and is an exciting medium to work in as you can make use of both text and visuals. You may wish to insert examples of your own work or research that has informed your area of practice.

Establishing a vlog

In addition to blogs, there is now the vlog, where you may choose to express your thoughts predominantly in video format. This is another exciting medium to access and express your thoughts, and your tutors may be able to assist you with this.

Disabled Students' Allowance (DSA)

- As a disabled student, you will have a support statement. You received this because medical information was provided by you or a family member to the university in the form of an application for Disabled Student's Allowance (DSA).

- DSA is additional funding to provide you with access to extra resources to enable you to engage in your course in the same way as other students who are not disabled.

> **Students: remember to buy course materials such as a folder for each subject/module, writing material, highlighter pens and notebooks.**

Tips for tutors

- Get to know the individual's preferred learning style. This may be ascertained in a tutorial (or regular tutorials) together with the student and their mentor/academic support worker(s). Whilst you should have access to the student's support statement to discuss with them as a guide, the above approach may make them feel more involved.

- Don't make any sudden changes e.g. to the timetable or coursework. Give the maximum notice possible if changes are unavoidable.

- Agree a process for a student if queries suddenly arise. For example, the student may wish to involve their mentor to help them manage their anxiety and work with you, the tutor, on a stepped plan to address the problem. So ensuring you have the mentor's contact email, if mutually agreed, would be a possible solution.

- Create clear lesson plans.

  - Provide some detail of each session and what to expect. This enables students to prepare and informs them whether discussion with other students will be required. This is key to lowering the anxiety of many students, allowing them to work to their advantage by focusing on skills.

  - It helps autistic students organise their time in instances where, for example, they may wish to enter/leave lecture theatres before others to avoid crowds and reduce sensory and social overload.

- Support workers can be invited to assist a student with discussion sessions if required, but discuss this with the student first.

- Lecture agendas.

  - These are helpful for all students, as they facilitate processing of information and enable better engagement in the activity. For example, this might include an introductory part, the main lecture and then a small group activity prior to feedback.

- Check that the student has understood e.g. by asking them to repeat the task requirements back and the timeline.

- Give a clear explanation about the handing in process and confirm this in emails.

- One-to-one meetings:

  - Time to process experiences is necessary. Allocate time after an event (good or bad) to discuss it with the student.

  - Regular setting of targets and dates throughout the course.

  - Individually-based solutions are essential as everyone has their own way of processing information and preferred way of communicating.

  - Space/time for a student to step out of a room to process things and compose themselves is really important, especially if a student suddenly finds themselves in a situation of extreme overload. If not appropriately addressed, this could result in a meltdown, which is extremely distressing for the student concerned. Discuss a strategy to help avoid this, as this helps the student manage difficult situations.

  - An allocated quiet room, or area where a student can remove themselves from unpleasant stimuli, is crucial. It allows the individual to maintain a sense of calm and perhaps continue with work in a different environment.

- Handouts

  - If these are part of the support statement, please let the student have them in good time prior to the lecture as it allows the student to process information, engage better with the course and to think of any questions.

- Final year

  - Particular clarity is required during the final year of university as the majority of autistic students and students with mental health problems will experience significant challenges in relation to the management of stress and anxiety.

  - Specific support plans regarding final hand-ins would be invaluable.

Tips for mentors and study skills support workers

- Check the student has a diary.

- Familiarise yourself with the student's timetable so as to schedule regular sessions (this may change in the early weeks).

- Discuss how the student likes to approach tasks/activities i.e. are they a visual learner, do they write lists or mind map?

- Check the course delivery addresses the student's support requirements e.g. the provision of handouts or slides on the Learning Management System (LMS) prior to the lecture.

- Check that the student is able to access lectures/seminars and is sitting in the best place for them, for instance to reduce disruption if they need to leave, and also to minimise the negative impact of others who may arrive late.

- Check a student's approach to assignments – set up a regular routine that is manageable. It will be different for individuals.

- Discuss whether a student wishes to have regular tutorials with you present.

- Group work is a particular stressor for students in the early days, and particularly for those who find initiating contact difficult, so be proactive in establishing a strategy for addressing this so as to reduce anxiety early on.

- Presenting in front of others can cause significant stress for some students, so discuss how they would like to approach this. Students with support statements can negotiate this.

- Establish a plan for accessing library resources in line with course work and assignments.

- Ensure that a plan for the student's final hand-ins is in place. This can be negotiated with the student and their tutor.

Part 2:
Exploring autism or mental well-being-related issues with or without your mentor

Chapter 3: Terminology

The terminology people use to refer to you is important. Confusion inevitably occurs since different people prefer different terminology, and when practitioners, such as tutors or disability workers, are not sure what you would like they may use terms that make you uncomfortable.

It is up to you what terminology you would like people to use.

So if they do not check with you, be clear and say something like:

- I have Asperger syndrome.
- I am on the autism spectrum.
- I am autistic.
- I have autism.
- I have high anxiety.
- I have general anxiety disorder.
- I have depression.

If it is difficult for you to say this to people, ask your mentor to help. You may never have thought about this as labels may just have been applied to you by practitioners.

Task for mentors: reflect on whether you are using the student's preferred form of communication to help them express themselves.

Different abilities do not make someone complex

It is not unusual for individuals to have a range of support requirements whether we are autistic, neurodivergent or non-autistic.

We all have support requirements... they are just different.

This does **not** make us complex. In fact, it is more reflective of human diversity

**We all need support at times, so
please don't call me COMPLEX
if you don't understand me...it's
mutual!**

Mentors: it is important to understand that using the word complex in relation to any student, and particularly one with unseen disabilities, masks the very real challenges and barriers they face on a daily basis. Even more, it prevents you as someone working with them from knowing how best to support them and work with them. **Ask** the student what terminology they prefer (Beresford, 2005, Graby, 2012, Kenny *et al*, 2015).

**Task for mentors: reflect on
whether you are using the student's
preferred form of communication
to help them engage with their
course and express themselves.**

Tips for mentors and study skills support workers

- This area may need to be revisited over the time of your work with the student due to their changing and developing identities.

- Try to keep up-to-date with language and terminology that autistic individuals are comfortable with using and be aware of those that trigger adverse reactions in individual students.

- Note that a student's identity will cover several areas so terminology may not be solely about autism. An awareness of intersectionality, therefore, is important, and Appendix 6 deals with some terminology that you and your student may wish to discuss.

Chapter 4: Friendships

Social activities and Facebook

The students' union at your university will have many clubs and societies, and any student can set up a new one.

■ At the beginning of the year, there is a 'fresher's fair', and you can join clubs and societies then.

■ If this is too overwhelming, you can go to the university website to check out the students' union societies online. This gives you time to process what you want to do at your own pace, and you can join up at any point throughout the year.

■ You can also go into the students' union office and talk to someone there.

■ Check to see if the group(s) you are interested in has a Facebook page. You can message someone via that to check for further information.

Developing a social network

How you do this depends very much on whether you want:

■ one or two close friends

■ a group of friends

■ someone on your course

■ different friends depending on interests and activities

■ geographical proximity e.g. if you want to meet them regularly, maybe a friend living near to you would be good.

Below are some things to think about when developing friendships, but remember, you may want to do things differently (Lawson, 2006b).

Interacting with new people

People have different preferences in relation to this. Do you prefer:

■ Face-to-face contact (some of us are good at this)?

■ Online contact (others of us prefer to communicate online)?

■ Or would you like to develop face-to-face contact with new friends, but need some support?

Below are some suggestions that people I have worked with have found useful:

- Decide why you want to communicate with someone first. Maybe it is because of a mutual interest; perhaps you wish to share and explore experiences of autism; alternatively you may wish to discuss your course. Try and be clear about what you want. It may be a mixture of these or other factors.

- Perhaps you have already been communicating with someone online for a while and you now wish to take this further. The thought of actually meeting and communicating face-to-face with someone can be daunting, so be open about this. The chances are that the other person could feel the same.

- If you say that you would like to meet, but that this is quite challenging for you, you might also find yourselves talking about this online for a while. This can help you both share and understand your similarities and differences, and perhaps you can support each other.

- Perhaps arrange to meet at a place you would both find interesting, so that if conversation becomes difficult, you can simply appreciate things around you e.g. an exhibition or a walk in the park.

- Your mentor could arrange linking you up and facilitate a first meeting, which they could attend.

Activity 4.1: Tell me about you and I'll tell you about me

This is a good icebreaker activity to get to know people in a number of settings, and it is fun to do. You can vary it according to the person you are with.

■ Place your hand on a piece of paper with the fingers spread wide apart.

■ Each of you then labels your digits as numbered below and places your hand next to the person you would like to find out more about:

  ■ Digit 1 is your name.

  ■ Digit 2 is where you are from.

  ■ Digit 3 is what subject you will be studying.

  ■ Digit 4 is something that you would like to tell the other person about yourself e.g. an interest.

  ■ Digit 5 is a place you have travelled to/would like to travel to.

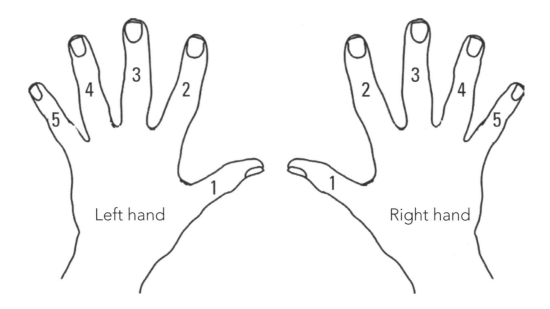

Adapt the activity according to your wishes/needs. You could take turns:

■ working your way through each digit

■ choosing which named digit you wish your partner to respond to in terms of providing information

■ working systematically, taking turns to provide information with each digit.

Activity 4.2: What makes a good friend? (see Appendix 3)

If you find the whole idea of developing a friendship(s) daunting, but would definitely like to do this, a good starting point can be in terms of deciding the qualities that are important to you in a person. Remember this can be added to or altered at any stage. Using Appendix 3 to help, you may wish to work alone or with your mentor to identify important personality traits that you would like or, conversely, would not like in a friend. Write them in the lists provided. These traits may be because they match or clash with your own, for example. Those traits you find interesting, and which you place in the middle column, are those which provide opportunity for discovering and building new friendships. With this information, you might then be able to identify certain social groups/ activities you might like to access.

Activity 4.3: Interests and activities (see Appendix 4)

You may have some specific interests and activities, and these are often an excellent starting point for helping you to engage with others. In addition, you may want to consider adding some new interests … university is a great place to do this.

One student described their experience of interacting with new people:

'Even now I still get social anxiety, but I push myself to talk to people because you never know what can come from a conversation and the friendships you can make. When starting university I struggled to find my tribe of people, so I set up my own tribe: Write Club. This was a place where people could come to write in a safe space and express themselves creatively. Because I had started my own group where we all had similar interests the pressure was off to socialise as I knew that everyone wanted to be there. Finding a mutual passion can be a great way to talk to someone and make new friends, because you can find yourself lost in a really interesting conversation and that can turn into a friendship you never expected. Also, trying something where you are out of your comfort zone can also help. In my second year I joined the university burlesque society, I didn't think I could be confident or sexy, but I realised that a lot of people who joined felt like they were in the same boat. Because we had such an inspirational dance teacher this helped us all flourish and have the confidence to perform and be part of successful shows and dance in the Birmingham Pride parade. I found myself naturally getting close to the people I was dancing with and met some incredible people who I will always hold fond memories of.'

Living with friends

You may find that you meet some new people that you like in your student accommodation, and many students stay in the same or different accommodation with this group the following year.

If you are living at home, but would like to live with friends, go to the chapter on independent living (Chapter 17) to help you work on these skills (if you need to) while you also build your friendships. Remember, living with others requires anyone to build skills of acceptance and understanding. Here is one student's experience:

> 'I found it enjoyable living with some of my friends, but there were issues with some because they didn't understand my habits and thought I was doing some things on purpose, when actually it was because of my Asperger's and dyspraxia (for example, saying inappropriate comments or spilling stuff and forgetting to clean up cutlery etc.). I also found it hard to communicate openly and have a face to face conversation (usually because it would involve eye contact) when trying to resolve conflict. This didn't help my friendships and created awkward tensions and upset for a long time, but eventually we were able to resolve things. However I had a lot of positive experiences living with my friends too, I got closer to some of them as a result of me confiding about my Asperger's, and it helped them to understand me more. They still treated me like a 'normal' human being, and we still had just as many laughs, inside jokes and fun times as all friends do.'

Discovering new activities

University has a serious side in that you are studying, but it is also fun too and is a time to discover new activities, whether you are studying in your home town or have moved away to study.

Many courses have activities in the early weeks to help you settle down with your course/module/tutor group and also investigate the area e.g. visits to museums or art galleries.

Spend some of your mentoring time looking at different websites with your mentor to help you identify activities to help you with your coursework and to build friendships.

> **A balance of coursework and fun is brilliant for stress management and developing a positive state of well-being.**

Tips for mentors and study skills support workers

- Do discuss what qualities a student considers make a good/bad friend.

- Do discuss with a student if they like to have friends.

- Do ask a student if they already have a friend or group of friends.

- Do discuss whether a student is making friends on the course as this can impact on aspects such as group work or making them feel isolated.

- It may be that the student is more comfortable with online friendships or that they would like to build up face-to-face friendships with support.

- Don't assume that a student will build friendships, has built friendships or even wants to build friendships in the same way as you. It may be that one-to-one or small group friendships work better or ones built on a mutual interest.

- Be prepared to discuss strategies for living with people with different habits which the student you support may find challenging. Look for solutions as this is a key life skill, and one which can be quite challenging.

- Work with students to extend their areas of interest and skills as this is also important for CV material.

Chapter 5:
Autism, mental health and self-awareness

**Remember...you are the expert
in you and your feelings.**

Sometimes it may be difficult expressing feelings, but in order for your mentor to help you settle into both the academic and social aspects of university life the two of you need to build a level of trust between you. Reflecting on the mentoring session may help you address points that you found good or those that were not so helpful. However, the following is worth keeping in mind:

■ You have a range of skills and abilities.

■ You also have some unseen, and certainly in many cases misunderstood, challenges.

■ Without support or meaningful strategies in place these challenges can act as barriers to your learning or to the development of your skills in order to contribute to society. These barriers can also make it difficult to function well or even at all in some situations.

■ It is helpful to discuss autistic traits as identified by yourself and others.

■ Think about your family tree: what are some identifying family traits?

Discussing the above with your mentor can help you express your individual identity and skills and tackle this in a way you feel is right for you.

Activity 5.1: My awareness diary

Keeping a journal of good and bad things about the week together with reasons behind them is really useful. For instance, it can be particularly important in helping you build a healthy lifestyle, in understanding patterns of 'what works for me', and identifying enabling and disabling environments.

Journals can be excellent for helping you to remember things if your memory is bad, and it can be fun to look back and see how things have progressed for you or what tools/strategies have worked.

There are four key areas you could reflect on:

■ Your course.

■ Your living environment (home, halls or student accommodation).

■ Your social life.

■ Your well-being.

Activity 5.2: Understanding how autism/mental health impacts on the individual

- Draw a picture of the body and label/describe or detail effects of autism and/or mental health on different parts your body. This helps to identify your strengths and weaknesses.

- Against each of these points, you may wish to work with your mentor on building some strategies (if you have not already done so).

- It may be useful to explore ways to voice the impact of mental well-being on your body and thinking about both the positive and negative feelings that you experience.

- Remember, the more familiar you are with the way your body reacts to things, the more control you have in your life.

Activity 5.3: Understanding my identity (1)

Draw an outline of a person.

- Add sticky notes around with comments on more general areas of your life such as skills, interests and feelings. For example:

  - What do you like to do e.g. play an instrument or do a sport?
  - Do you enjoy watching a team sport?
  - Do you have a professional skill you are developing e.g. composition, a visual art, engineering?
  - Do you have a hobby?
  - What would you like others to know about you in terms of your identity?

Activity 5.4: Understanding my identity (2)

Do a mind map of things that make you who you are, such as:

- activities you enjoy

- things you do not like

- aspects of your disability that are important

- gender

- faith.

Remember, autism/mental health is only part of your identity. On its own it does not define you.

It is important, for this reason, to raise awareness about autism/Asperger's syndrome and mental health, because they are hidden disabilities, and need to be explained. So as you do this activity, think about:

■ Issues such as sensory sensitivity, likes, dislikes (Jackson, 2006; Shore, 2006).

■ Disclosure (Moxon, 2006; Murray, 2006).

■ Gender/identity issues (Bornstein, 2013; Lawson, 2005; 2006a).

Tips for mentors and study skills support workers

■ Assist students to develop reflective skills regarding themselves and their week as it is the foundation to them extending self-awareness and (for many) having more control over their life.

■ Help the student to separate their life into main areas so as not to become overwhelmed by problems should they arise.

■ For a student, being able to identify how autism/mental well-being impacts on them physically and mentally is a key part of being able to engage successfully with the course and to build friendships. Activities identified in this chapter, and other activities you may introduce, will assist with confidence and being able to explain what they find to be an enabling environment. This is essential for all students.

■ Some students may not be comfortable with their autism diagnosis. Be sensitive to how individuals identify and the key targets they wish to set for mentoring sessions.

■ Be prepared to discuss and address other identities a student has. This is crucial if issues relating to gender and sexual orientation are raised as signposting to outside services may be wanted/required.

■ Ensure a balance to your work with your student(s). Focus your session on their skills, abilities and areas of interests. Maybe look at new ones they may wish to begin at home, university or in another venue.

■ Distress often indicates a requirement for additional support, be prepared to discuss this and suggest that you may need to ask the disability support worker for advice regarding additional resources available on site.

Chapter 6:
Sensory sensitivity and sensory overload

It is critical that the individual (autistic) student, their mentor and others working alongside them understand the distinction between being sensitive to a specific sensory stimulus and being hyper- or hypo-sensitive to sensory triggers.

All triggers can impede engagement with activities or even prevent an individual from functioning as they would wish, and can be exacerbated by sensory overload. The following activity incorporates some reactions/issues that have been raised in sessions with me over the years and is by no means definitive. It provides you with an opportunity to explore your own responses, so remember that your experience matters and may be different.

Sensitivities

Sound

- Sudden noises may cause alarm.

- Sudden noises can be distracting.

- High-pitch sounds can be painful.

- The sound of fluorescent lighting or air-conditioning can be distracting.

Light

- Brightness can cause sensory overload.

- Light frequency can affect individuals differently, e.g. the Hz frequency from strobe or LED lighting may cause seizures or migraines.

- Bright backgrounds on slides can make these difficult to read.

- 'Busy' backgrounds or slides can be difficult to process.

Touch

- Being touched may be painful.

- An exception to this may be if contact has been asked for.

- The amount of pressure being applied is also important.

- Unpredictable touch is particularly painful, even just resting your hand on someone's arm or shoulder.

- Being touched by an unfamiliar person can cause pain, alarm and confusion.

Talk to your mentor or tutor about this. It may be possible to ensure that you sit in a certain part of the lecture room to minimise you being bumped into.

Temperature

Heating can be problematic as it affects concentration, and it is important to deal with so that you can enjoy what you are studying and focus on the lecture. There may also be others who find the temperature disagreeable, so never be afraid to let someone know. You could:

- Move to a different seat.
- Open/close the window.
- Talk to your mentor/study buddy.
- Talk to your tutor. Both should be able to address this.

Smell

- A smell in the room may make the student want to leave the room/building and to run away from it.
- Perfumes and cleaning products can be overpowering.
- If the environment is not clean, it may not be possible for the student to work.

Taste

- Sensitivity to certain types of foods (texture and smell) can also impact on taste.
- Go for simple foods.
- Prepare your own foods and bring them in.

Kinaesthetic

- You may be slightly 'clumsy' or have dyspraxia, so if tactile, practical sessions are your preferred style of learning, and staff need to understand that sessions need to be delivered in such a way that you can engage.
- Your mentor can help.

Hunger and thirst

- Managing sudden or extreme hunger or thirst can be really difficult as it is both distracting and can impact on your ability to function well.

- Being proactive is an excellent coping strategy. Try and make it a habit to always carry a drink and some snacks with you, especially those that are high in energy.

Time to process experiences

Sensory overload can mount up quite quickly and it is critical to put strategies in place to help avoid or minimise this:

- Set up/identify a quiet area.

- Spend a few minutes doing nothing each day.

- Use full-spectrum or daylight-stimulating bulbs.

- Meditation.

- Yoga.

- Calm music.

> **Mentors, tutors and any other support workers need to help an autistic student experiencing sensory overload in a calm manner.**

Activity 6.1: Identify triggers and solutions

Think about all the different senses and how they impact on you.

- Write a list.

- Notice in what environments these tend to occur/or are worse.

- Try not to worry if these seem 'odd'. The world is oriented towards the requirements of non-autistic people, so your reactions are important.

- Have you developed any strategies?

- Let you mentor/tutor know so that they can support you.

Advice for support staff and tutors

One or more experiences of sensory overload occurring together or in very quick succession may be enough to trigger an inability to function or a meltdown. In these moments, it may be impossible for an autistic student to verbalise what they need, so be observant, reduce lighting, noise, strong smells etc. Try to move others away in order to give the student more space. If this is not possible, keep speaking calmly to the student to reassure them, and when the student is less distressed take them to a quiet area.

At a later date check with the student as to whether they would find the Autistic Space Kit (ASK) useful as a tool to cope with stress and anxiety (see Chapter 19): http://www.autisticspacekit.co.uk.

Remember ... it is usually not helpful to ask a student in extreme distress if they are ok!
They are not.

Be proactive and work with them to put some coping strategies in place.

Tips for mentors and study skills support workers

- Be proactive as sensory overload can have a significant and sudden adverse impact on some individuals.

- Discuss any sensory triggers that students may have, and perhaps mention other triggers that you are aware of as students often struggle to talk about this area. Knowing that other people struggle with sensory overload is quite empowering.

- Consider whether specific sensory stimuli impedes a student's coursework, their ability to access university or their ability to function more generally e.g. lighting, noise or dirty environments.

- Students may benefit from alerting tutors to any sensitivities. So discuss this with them and draw together a plan should the need arise.

- Establishing a daily (or more frequent) quiet time is important to calming the nerves. Talk with students about building a range of different activities into their day/week.

- Identify quiet spaces/break out rooms around the university.
- Familiarise yourself with the Autistic Space Kit (ASK) app (http://www. autisticspacekit.co.uk/) as many students may be unaware of it. It is a well-planned tool designed by autistic individuals for autistic individuals to assist with managing anxiety.

Chapter 7:
Managing stress and anxiety

Managing stress and anxiety is an important aspect of dealing with your well-being generally and more specifically. This can be stress that relates to the environment or stress that you experience inside you, and that can be controlled in certain ways. This section explores both.

Ways of coping with stress

Identifying quiet areas

Becoming familiar with the layout of the university can really work to your advantage. Instead of feeling rushed because you are unsure how to get from one lecture room to a room where you are having a seminar, for example, walking around the university when it is quieter can allow you to establish the best route for you. Perhaps consider the following strategies:

- Get to the lecture room early when it is not so busy.

- Identify a seat where you are most comfortable and there are less distractions.

Managing positive flow states

Switching your focus to the management of positive flow states (or the mental state of being completely present and fully immersed in a task), can lead to a happier sense of well-being. If you have a sense of well-being the following is likely to be true:

- You are engaged in a doable task.

- You are able to focus.

- You have a clearly established goal.

- Immediate feedback is provided.

- You can move without worrying.

- You have a sense of control.

- The sense of self is suspended as you are engaged in the task.

- You have temporarily lost a sense of time.

(Krueger, 2015)

However, becoming lost in an individual task is not just what positive flow is really about. It exists alongside a balance of individual tasks and those which involve others, not necessarily large groups, but people who enjoy a similar activity (see Chapter 4).

Breathing and relaxation

It is helpful to know how our breathing is when we are feeling more relaxed and happy, so the following activities will help in this respect. Also, they will help you identify changes in your breathing or any physiological changes in relation to specific feelings/emotions or states of mind.

> **Remember: the more familiar you are with your different patterns of breathing and accompanying physiological sensations, the more control you have over these.**

Unhelpful connections

Time to process experiences is necessary in order to make sense of the present moment and not link it to past experiences. The latter may or may not have had a positive impact on you.

Opportunities to discuss experiences with your mentor will help you to work through any worries or concerns. These opportunities are generally lacking within the HE environment, so if you have a mentor, this is one way that you may choose to relate to them.

Past bad experiences may leave some students with a real fear of making mistakes, and this is unfortunate since we learn best from our mistakes (Robinson, 2010; Robinson, 2006).

There is also often high anxiety experienced about 'fitting in', and this is often based on false perceptions of what this might be. Again, discussing this with your mentor or with other students, particularly those with similar experiences, will be helpful in exploring this area of anxiety (Brown *et al*, 2015).

Breathing and anxiety

Practising deep breathing is essential for dealing with anxiety. However, many of us think we are breathing deeply, when in fact we are only really breathing at a shallow level. For this reason, it is useful to draw your attention to the difference between shallow breathing and deep breathing so that you can practise these when you are not stressed and then more quickly pick up on this in moments of stress.

Shallow breathing

This is the breathing we use as a flight or fight response, and when we are under stress or very anxious. It is also known as 'over breathing' or hyperventilation and enables us to increase the oxygen (O2) in our bloodstream and lower the carbon dioxide (CO2). Shallow breathing occurs when we breathe only as far as the throat, and an example of this is a dog panting; quick shallow breaths. Lowering the CO2 level in the bloodstream can cause several different effects, which may be:

- feeling peculiar, dizzy, or a bit faint
- disturbances of vision
- twitches in your face
- tingling in your hands and feet
- spasms or cramping in your hands and feet.

Deep breathing

Deep breathing is the breathing we use when we are relaxed. It is the breathing we see in people who are sleeping peacefully, and is the breathing that helps us deal with anxieties, keep our heads clear, enable us to think and react in a more controlled way. Deep breathing occurs when we breathe right down into our abdomen and can see this rise and fall in the stomach. Deep lungfuls of fresh air can calm you down, and in addition, it can boost your immune system.

Practising the following exercises several times a day helps you become more aware of your breathing and enables you to be more in control in situations that make you anxious.

Sitting or standing up straight with your feet hip width apart,

1. Place your hand on your throat and 'pant' five times, breathing through your mouth. This is shallow breathing.

2. Now place your hand on your chest, and breathe in through your nose to a count of four, hold your breath for two, then breathe out through your mouth for six counts. Repeat this five times, watching your hand rise and as your lungs fill with air and empty as you breathe out.

3. Finally, place your hand on your abdomen and breathe in through your nose lowering your breathing down into your abdomen. Watch your hand rise and fall. For a few minutes, breathe in for four counts, hold your breath for two and breathe out for six counts. Notice how your body becomes more relaxed, your thoughts still and clearer, and your anxiety lessens.

Do-in massage

This is a type of self-massage based on shiatsu (acupressure) which you can do on yourself while breathing deeply. It is based on channels in the body where energy passes through, and which in times of stress may become blocked and cause tension. Do-in massage (pronounced *doh-in*) can help you relieve this tension and feel more relaxed.

It is best if you wear loose comfortable clothing to help you really relax.

1. Stand with your feet hip-width apart and feet facing forwards. Arms hang loosely by your side.

2. Take a deep breath in, raise your arms and 'brush' the ceiling, twisting your wrists. Let your arms drop and breathe out. Repeat.

3. Make your wrists floppy, tap your head from front to back. Then smooth your forehead. Using your thumb, make circular movements along the upper then lower parts of your eye socket.

4. Using your middle finger, make circular movements from the corner of your eye down each side of your nose. Continue under your cheekbones until you reach just behind your ear.

5. Next, make circular movements across your upper lip and then your lower lip and chin, finally pinching along your jaw and out to your ears.

6. Pinching your earlobe with your thumb and forefinger, make circular movements and gradually work up along the outer part of the ear.

7. Holding your right elbow in your left hand, gently massage the left side of your neck and shoulder. Make a loose fist with your right hand and gently tap the top left side of your back. Repeat on the other side.

8. With a loose right fist, tap down the outside of your left arm and up the inside (twice). Then with your right thumb and fingers, gently massage your wrist and hand, working between the bones. With the index and middle finger of the right hand, work each finger and the thumb of the left hand in a circular motion, pull, and shake your right hand out. Repeat on other side.

9. Make loose fists with each hand, and taking a deep breath, fling your arms out wide, then as you exhale, pummel your chest with your fists.

10. Bend forwards from the hips and exhale. With loose fists, tap your back from as high as you can reach down to your tailbone. Then pummel your buttocks.

11. Tap down the back of both legs and up the inside.

12. Sit down on the floor with your legs out-stretched. Bend your right knee, drop your knee to the side and take your right foot in your hands. Gently massage your ankle bones and around your heel. Then work in small circular movements with both thumbs, along the sole of your foot. At the same time, use your fingers to work between the bones on the upper part of the foot

13. Finally, lie down flat on the floor with your legs slightly apart and your arms relaxed slightly away from your body and by your side. Breathe deeply down into your abdomen and feel the weight of your body sinking into the floor. Do this for a few minutes. Then slowly roll onto your left side, gently raise yourself into a kneeling position still breathing deeply. When you are ready, gradually stand up and gently shake yourself out.

Sensory-awareness techniques

Pamper your feet.

At the end of a day, give yourself a treat and relax by soaking your feet in warm water, then massage them with a combination of essential oils or a moisturiser.

Activity 7.1: Paying attention to eating

I like to call this 'Zenning with a Raisin', but you can also do this with some pieces of chocolate. You can do this 5-10 minutes each day.

You will need: several raisins/pieces of chocolate, pen and paper. Turn your mobile off. Spend around 30 seconds on each stage:

1. **Hold** the raisin in your hand.
   Notice its weight and shadow.

2. **Look** at the raisin.
   Explore every part of it: shades and highlights; textures - folds and ridges.

3. **Hold** it between thumb and forefinger.
   How does it feel? Explore its texture through touch.

4. **Smell** the raisin.
   Does it have a smell? What is the smell like? If it has no smell, then notice this.

5. **Place** the raisin on the tongue.
   Notice hand and arm movements. Notice what the tongue does. Explore the sensations of having the raisin on your tongue. Explore the raisin with your tongue and notice the sensations.

6. **Bite** into the raisin.
   Notice the effects on the raisin and in your mouth. Notice tastes released. Notice the texture of the raisin as you bite and chew. Notice differences, changes and sensations in the mouth.

7. **Swallow.**
   Notice when you first need to swallow. Notice the movement and position of the tongue. Notice sensations of swallowing the raisin as it moves down into your stomach. Notice how many times you swallow and the movements of your tongue after swallowing.

8. **After-effects.**
   Is there an after taste? What is the sensation of having no raisin in the mouth? Do you automatically want another one?

(Williams & Penman, 2011)

Activity 7.2: Noticing the good things in our lives

It is important that we re-train our brains using our senses as our natural survival mechanism is wired to remember negative experiences thereby protecting us from these in the future. This easily allows us to catastrophise the whole day instead of seeing the reality, where there was a combination of good, bad and neutral events.

> **Train the memory to focus on the good events in your day by focusing on these for a few seconds at a time and allowing these to build into a store of positive, life-enriching experiences.**

Activity 7.3: Using your senses to pay attention

Any event that is good, however small, that happens in your day, pay attention to and note down. This may be the calm atmosphere walking alongside the canal at night, or the smell of the coffee that you make in the morning.

Strategies for reacting to 'change'

Change can be difficult to handle, so it helps to have some tried and tested tools and strategies in your collection that you are familiar with, and that help you when you are at your most stressed. Consider the following options:

1. **Immediacy:** a stress ball or object that you have in your pocket that you can use to 'ground you' and help you focus.

2. **Familiarity:** make yourself familiar with what exactly it is about change that causes your anxiety. There will be many similarities and differences among students, and understanding your experiences helps you maintain a sense of control. Every individual has different experiences. Here is what one student recommends:

> 'I have always struggled with change, such as moving house, changing school and moving to university. I would say I have learnt a lot through one of the biggest changes that I encountered: moving from one place to another. I was completely out of my comfort zone and ended up being really unhappy there. The second time I went to university I decided to go to somewhere closer, somewhere I was familiar with. It might not be possible to always work or study somewhere that you are familiar with, but that doesn't mean you can't visit there and get used to the place before you move. My second piece of advice is to choose a passion to focus on. While at my first university, even though I was studying nursing I found my passion for creative writing. This helped me to realise I was in the wrong place and needed to be in Birmingham. Whilst at my second university, I invested myself in lots of creative societies, and with likeminded people, and even though it took until February the next year to find the right people for me, I finally felt like I could settle somewhere. This then led on to me living with friends in my final year and I am now living with my partner and have a job working in the students' union. I would say invest yourself in many different things and you will transition more smoothly rather than when you are trying to force it. Remember to be open-minded and if you know you struggle with big change try gradual change first and work your way up from there.'

Anxiety strategies – maintaining a level of calm

I am a firm believer in mind mapping activities as a visual tool to assist breaking down issues into their components. It is particularly useful to do this when feeling overwhelmed by emotions to do with a number of different factors, and which seem to be unhelpfully blurring into one big mess. The good news is that this can be sorted out.

Stress relievers: stress balls, stones and crystals

There is an abundance of these that you can buy in shops or online, and they are great to keep in your pocket or bag for those moments when you find yourself becoming quite stressed or anxious.

Experiment with those that work for you and leave some lying around your house or room within easy reach. You may want to set up a calm area, placing the items that help you most in a place where you focus on them at the end of a day or in moments of anxiety.

Essential oils and candles

Another thing that may help those who are not over-sensitive to smells to relax is essential oils. You can buy a range of burners that plug in or those that use candle lights (depending on whether you are in a hall of residence). Alternatively, you can sprinkle some over your bedcover to relax you.

Music and relaxation

How about putting on some calming music and trying the following activity?

> **Working from your forehead down to your toes, screw up and release each part independently, so that you are tensing and relaxing each area of your body. Try to separate out each area and release each part independently e.g. each part of your face, arm, wrist and hand.**
>
> **Notice the difference as you relax, and see if your mind is more peaceful.**

Evening wind-down

Evening activities can be quite mentally stimulating as this is the way in which you can distract yourself from daily stressors. This often includes hours spent on online games or social media. However, this does not provide you with any wind down time, and it is important for your well-being to find a good way of getting you into snooze mood. It is important not only to have enough sleep, but to have good quality sleep.

Activity 7.4: Stream of thought

- In moments of extreme anxiety, when it is difficult to calm the mind, take a piece (or several pieces) of paper, and without consciously picking and choosing what you write, note down everything that comes to mind in a flowing stream of uncontrolled thought.

- Keep writing until your mind eventually becomes still. It will, but this may take several pieces of paper.

- At a later stage (in a day or so), look back on these thoughts you expressed (do this on your own or with someone you trust) and reflect on whether there are any patterns.

- This may help you to plan strategies to cope with anxiety in the future. You could use your mentor, a trusted friend or a family member to help you.

> **You may now feel tired, so slow your body down by listening to some soothing music, doing a breathing and grounding activity or reading a book.**

Activity 7.5: Balancing your thoughts

Having engaged in Activity 7.3, it is quite important to balance your thoughts and to try to do this in a more controlled way. You might find it useful to try the following:

- For each negative thought that you wrote down previously, counter it with a positive thought.

- As before, reflect on this, maybe a few days later.

- Again, you could discuss this with your mentor, a friend or family member.

- Use this to build strategies and become more aware as to how anxiety impacts on you.

Activity 7.6: Drawing your worries (Appendix 5 provides an example)

On a piece of paper, start to map out your worries.

- Try putting your worries into separate circles or boxes
- Can you 'chunk' these under themes?

- Can you identify any links between these?

- Perhaps draw an arrow between those that you believe have a connection.

- Visualising your worries like this can help you break them down and not become overwhelmed by them.

- You may want to discuss this map with someone you trust. By explaining it, you can often make better sense of your worries. Also you gain a different perspective if the other person asks questions to clarify what you are saying.

Activity 7.7: Plan your worries

Worrying can waste a lot of time that could be better spent and can drain you of energy. It also detracts from developing creativity and engaging in tasks and activities. All these are a very good reason to try this activity.

> **Allocate a certain amount of time at the end of each day. It is useful if this is the same time each day in order to establish a routine. This time can then be devoted to sorting through your worries.**
>
> **When the time is up, stop worrying and do something else.**

Activity 7.8: Sleep assessor - tick any which apply to you

This activity is about you reflecting on key points in order to build some healthy daily habits that encourage sleep. You may wish to work on this with your mentor to add some additional points that you would find useful. This is your tool, so if you use it you can adapt it to suit you, so if none of the points work for you, replace them by something that does.

An approximately fixed time for going to bed.

An approximately fixed time for waking up.

No alcohol in the four hours before sleep.

No caffeine in the four hours before sleep.

No heavy eating in the four hours before sleep.

Regular daytime exercise (but not just before bed).

Clean, comfortable bed and bedding.

Quiet, peaceful room for sleeping.

Bed at comfortable temperature.

A peaceful bedtime routine without excess stimulation.

Anxiety and its link to other emotions

Anger

Whilst working with many different autistic people over the years, there has often been a consistent explanation as to why somebody feels angry. Without even asking people directly, regular conversations and listening to individual students' opinions and concerns frequently points to a lack of opportunity to be heard, either within the home environment or at school.

Here are some techniques that I have found really useful with individuals, and which they often enjoy as it involves them leading the conversation about the barriers they face:

- Developing talks and presentations.
- Presenting poetry and other creative writing.
- Explaining challenges faced in their specific subject area e.g. many autistics have perfect singing pitch and will find it irritating practising next to someone who does not.

Fear

Fear and anger can be readily interwoven. We can be scared of the unknown or change, or once we have had one bad experience we may generalise this to other areas. Either way, breaking fear down into manageable parts is crucial to its understanding.

Holiday panic

Holiday situations are often a cause of anxiety for a number of reasons. These may include, but are not limited to, the following, so let's explore each one of these in turn and look at some ways of coping with them. Remember you can add to these or adjust them according to your preferences.

Lack of structure

Going from a term-time structure to a more relaxed holiday one, where you are freer to do what you wish, can be quite daunting. To manage this look at the skills at your disposal that you can tap into:

■ A weekly time management sheet (Appendix 2). This is useful in providing an overview of your whole week.

■ A daily time management sheet (Appendix 1). This gives you a more detailed description.

■ Interests you like to pursue and explore these further.

■ New interests you would like to pursue. Maybe you have some activities you have not had time to engage with. The holidays are a good time for this. Maybe they would add to and compliment your course, or perhaps they are separate from this.

■ Building independent living skills. The holidays are always a good time to build on your independent living skills. For a start, you will probably have more time as you do not have the pressures of course deadlines. So try to ensure that you include these in your planning e.g. tidy room, go to the shops, cooking (maybe to help others).

Managing change at home

Predicting events

■ Calendars are extremely useful so that you can see family activities and events if you are living at home. You can incorporate these into your own weekly/daily planner.

■ Ask your family to add to this as soon as they know of a new upcoming event to give you time to process your week/day.

Being around family members in the home

This can be tricky for anybody, but more so when you need time to yourself for whatever reason. And remember, we do have a right to have this time; it allows us to recharge our batteries, to relax, and to process the happenings of the day. Perhaps consider the following:

■ Do you have your own room? If so, ask others to respect your space.

- If they need to come into your room, you could ask them to knock and wait for an answer; or agree when they can come in and for what reason.

- Perhaps you can get them what they need, or put your laundry in a basket outside your room (better still, try and learn to do it yourself).

Visiting specific situations

Family events often bring with them activities which you may find stressful. Frequently environments non-autistic people find fun can be full of challenges regarding sensory and social overload for autistic people or those with mental health challenges. One such environment is restaurants, often booked for celebrations. However, the advent of the internet has made it possible to look at the layout of a restaurant/venue online and also to look at a menu. So if you find visiting a restaurant challenging, here are a few tips:

- Look at the restaurant's website and check its layout.

- Is there anywhere specific that you would find easier to sit? If so, ask someone to reserve seating e.g. not by a busy door, away from bright light, or in a quieter part of the restaurant.

- You may find it difficult to eat certain food, so have a look at the menu (there may be a few, so check with the person booking the place which one will be used).

- Most chefs are more than happy to prepare food for an individual who has food intolerance/allergies or simply limited preferences. If you can, let them know in advance, or get someone to help you.

Identify stressful family situations

Students live in a variety of accommodation, and some of you may still be living at home. Whilst this may be the cheaper option, it may not always be the best if there are significant family tensions. These may be for a range of reasons, but some that I have come across include:

- Wanting more independence in terms of flexible meal times, privacy, money management etc.

- Expressing a wish for support (not 'meddling' as it has often been experienced) to develop independent living skills, but parents not wanting to accept that their 'child' needs to learn these.

- Lack of acceptance of an individual's expressed identity.

- Bullying and domestic violence in the family home.

- Sexual abuse from someone entering the family home.

- Imposed terminology.

- An inability by family to see the individual student's skills and abilities; rather there is an insistence that the student is somehow dysfunctional and therefore requires support for this reason.

- Adapting to and managing a changed lifestyle at university and fitting this into a more familiar one at home can lead to tensions.

All of the above, and other reasons, can cause stress. Highlight these issues to your mentor, and they can help you plan some coping strategies before things become overwhelming.

A different experience voiced by one student is as follows:

> 'Whilst studying at university I went through one of the hardest changes at home you can go through, namely a house repossession. During my time at university I was commuting and helping to support my mum and brother through this difficult time. In order to cope with the stress at home I made use of the counselling services at university, I was in and out of these services, but I found in particular my last two counsellors to be the most helpful. They made me challenge my own negative belief system and helped me make some positive life changes after my most recent traumatic experience at home. I also found that doing creative things helped me express and channel my emotions, such as writing, performing and dancing at burlesque. I found that when having a difficult time at home, the most important thing to do was to keep going to things. In my first year, I struggled to attend my classes as the stress at home increased, but because of the Write Club society on Wednesdays I had something regular to motivate myself to go to every week. I told myself this was an achievement, even though I couldn't bring myself to go in to seminars I was at least still doing something I enjoyed and it kept me writing for my degree. In my second year when things were getting really bad I had built up my support network at university, and it got to the point where I didn't have enough money to travel home. Luckily because I had made friends through similar creative interests I had a place to stay so I didn't have to worry about being able to afford to travel to university every day. I continued to expand my creative network by making friends in the BCU burlesque society where it also became something regular that I would attend. Whenever I would have a hard time at home or in the day it was the perfect way to de-stress,

by dancing and laughing with friends. I am glad that at the start of my second year I aimed to try new things because it kept me going right until the end of my degree.'

> **Remember … dealing with problems early on makes life less stressful and reduces anxiety.**

Tips for mentors and study skills support workers

- Be proactive and introduce some strategies at the outset. It would be reasonable to assume a certain level of anxiety among a new student or a student new to you.

- Discuss triggers and a range of strategies that your student would like to practise regularly e.g. calm breathing, drawing or a sport.

- Fundamental to any student is establishing effective strategies for managing stress and anxiety. This book introduces some, and I would encourage you to collect your own that you are familiar with and that your individual students like. Everyone's preferences are different.

- Strategies need to be both readily accessible, e.g. breathing, and also daily, e.g. going for a walk.

- Help students build a plan to manage holiday periods as these can bring additional stress and worry and discuss reasons behind this e.g. changing environments, social events, a fear of lack of support.

- Look at ways to manage avoiding unhelpful or triggering people.

- Visit sleeping patterns regularly with students who find sleep difficult. Often patterns of behaviour established to help cope with wakefulness are not conducive to sleep, so an assessment of this area is really useful.

- Make links with the student between their sleep and work patterns and production. It is useful to determine what is helping and what is not, and it is often difficult to do this on your own.

Chapter 8:
Communication

Everyone has their own individual style of communication and their own communication preference(s). For example:
- **Using visuals.**
- **Written text.**
- **Text + visuals.**
- **Various software techniques.**
- **Using a range of media.**

Recently more attention has been paid to autistic people, with the following areas typically being raised and causing a lot of resultant distress:

- Being misunderstood.
- Being interpreted as direct and rude.
- Being thought of as rude for lack of eye contact.

These issues have been raised by many autistic writers, and Milton (2012) has described this state of 'you don't understand us, and we don't understand you' as the double empathy problem.

Communication can be challenging for autistic people as it can be easier to focus on what they want to talk about rather than actually joining in the conversation. Therefore turn-taking in conversations can be difficult. In addition, this is perhaps not as simplistic as it may seem, since a difficulty in beginning and ending conversations can further perpetuate the problem, thus resulting in an individual continuing to follow their own conversational thread.

Understanding the impact of autism/mental health problems

Your experiences as an autistic individual will have elements that are both similar and different to other autistics. However, many students I have worked with have expressed worries about being made to feel different. This is also true of those students experiencing mental health challenges.

Tackling isolation and making friends.

Finding others to talk to is critical. If you find it difficult joining a group or making contacts, ask your mentor/support worker to help you.

Expressing differences and needs (using a range of methods: visual and verbal)

You may have already tried connecting with other autistics via the internet, or through autistic-led groups such as Autscape (see Chapter 22). This is important in helping you make friends with others who may experience similar challenges to you, either in the same way or differently. The earlier chapter (Chapter 4) on friendships has several suggestions for ways to make friends. In addition, activities here will help you realise that differences are good!

Emotions book: self and others

Everyone processes emotions differently.

Trying to talk about your emotions can be really difficult, and sometimes using a visual image to explain them can help, especially when we are trying to voice how others can make us feel. This can be done yourself or with a mentor or someone else you trust.

Tackling complex and confusing emotions is more easily done if you try to break down experiences into component parts, allocating a feeling or emotion to each.

Activity 8.1: Creating an emotions book

Creating a book to work on emotions using text and visuals (drawings, photos, magazine clips) allows you to reflect on experiences using a range of different media. Whilst similar to the narrative diary activity overleaf, this activity focuses solely on emotions, contextualising these and attaching them to different life experiences. This is useful in identifying differences and similarities in your own reactions to situations and enables you to build confidence and self-esteem by planning coping strategies where necessary. As a starting point, some key emotions you may choose to work on are:

■ happiness

■ shyness

■ affection

- anxiety (see section below)

- depression

- anger.

This is by no means a definitive list, and you can work alone or with your mentor to identify other emotions that you struggle to express.

Activity 8.2: Photomontage

Visual thinkers might like to indulge in this activity by way of exploring certain aspects of their past or present life that they wish to 'voice' or express. You can start a photomontage from many different points … choose one that suits you.

> **One thing's for sure…as soon as you think you have finished, there is always another thought that you can add. This can lead to the expression of your voice through lots of creative artwork.**

- Write a list of things that you want to express, or inform others about.

- Draw a mind map of issues that you want to share.

- Maybe then collect cuttings from newspapers/magazines, photos, text or poetry that you can start arranging in a draft form in your collage.

- You might feel confident enough to start the main collage straight away.

The collage (or photomontage if it is an arrangement of photographic material) can help with communication in a variety of ways:

- Expressing difficulties visually may help discussion and understanding with your mentor, who will be in a better position to help you communicate matters to relevant others e.g. tutors.

- Visual exploration of thoughts and feelings can enable your understanding of these and allow you to unravel them if they are overwhelming. You can then explain these to others.

- It acts as a point of discussion, drawing those who have less experience of autism/mental health challenges into a conversation which is specific to you. This is advantageous in that the discussion is focused, as opposed to generalised to all autistic individuals, and you are placed as the expert in your life experiences.

- It can permit your exploration of specific themes, such as friendships or employment, looking for preferences or potential areas of difficulty.

Activity 8.3: Narrative diary

Storying your life is one way of expressing yourself and exploring aspects of your life that have had an impact on you. You may find it fun to do a narrative diary, and this can be used for yourself or to share snippets of your life with others. This can comprise photos, drawings, poetry, text, newspaper cut-outs or almost anything that has shaped your past and brought you to be the person you are today.

As something that can be done over time, this medium allows for reflection and processing and will be an invaluable resource if you wish to share specific information with others at university. An example of why you might wish to do this is if you have found that certain aspects of your past trigger overwhelming experiences that you find difficult to put into words alone. It can be cathartic looking back on this type of resource and noticing how your life journey has progressed.

Enabling environments

Knowing what type of environment you work best in will enable you to find spaces where you are able to work comfortably and well at the university. In addition, working with your mentor so that you can communicate this to your tutors will help them understand your support requirements.

Are these spaces with dimmer lights, less noise, or maybe they are less crowded? Perhaps particular smells make it difficult for you to concentrate? Or maybe the lighting and data projector in the lecture theatres hum constantly? Either way, let someone know, since if you are unable to concentrate, then you cannot work to your best and your grades will ultimately be lower than you deserve.

Activity 8.4: Communicating your enabling environments

If you find it difficult to communicate what environments you find more enabling, it is sometimes easier to focus on a specific place and to put what works and what does not into a PowerPoint slide presentation. Think about aspects of your department or course:

- What aspects work?
- What aspects are more disabling and do not allow you to function at your best?
- Use each slide to address a separate point e.g. sensory overload.

- What is it about your course that triggers sensory overload in you? Do you have a suggestion as to how this could be changed? Work with your mentor on this.

- Your disability advisor/disability support worker should have addressed a lot of this in your support statement, but you have more control if you are able to be even more specific.

- This activity is also useful when you are looking for employment.

The university has a duty to make reasonable adjustments, but it cannot do this if you do not advise them about your requirements.

Tips for mentors and study skills support workers

- Introduce the agenda to mentoring/study skills sessions if you have not already done so. This can be visual, a list, a mind map or whatever format a student finds helpful.

- Use the agenda to shape the conversation and points to address or to work on for the next session.

- Introduce plenty of turn taking into the conversation as students will have to do this in group work and it is an important life and social skill.

- Discuss a range of possible social conversation openers and ways to finish a social conversation that work for your students in a range of contexts. These provide a way to help some individuals settle in some situations, although others may find this irritating as situations are hypothetical. The emphasis is therefore on what works for the individual.

- Discuss how your student may wish to communicate with their tutor e.g. by email or in a weekly one-to-one tutorial to address concerns.

- Since friendships can be problematic, discuss different groups run by the students' union as these provide a range of ways of accessing an activity and communicating with people through a shared interest.

- Being able to express emotions and feelings can be challenging, so often the use of mixed media can be helpful. Consider working on a scrapbook or narrative diary with a student to map events and feelings. This will facilitate conversation.

Chapter 9:
Disclosure – a personal choice

This is a matter that comes up in various guises, such as socially, in relation to your course and peers, or regarding future employment. It is therefore important to look at a number of key areas:

■ Why is disclosure important?

■ Who would you want to tell?

■ Why would you want to tell them?

■ How much do you need to say?

Unless you just want to tell everybody details regarding your identity, which may not solely relate to autism/mental health, you might want to consider the above questions. They give a sense of purpose to the conversation, and instead of feeling pressured into telling people why you might do things in the way that you do (and there is no reason that you should be), reflecting on these areas gives you the chance to take control over any conversation. See the previous chapter on communication with some ideas as to how to approach this. In addition, you may wish to read the book 'Coming Out Asperger: diagnosis, disclosure and self-diagnosis' by Murray (2006), a collection of varied experiences from other autistic people.

Positive reasons to disclose

Whilst there still remain many barriers to inclusion experienced by disabled people, being aware of your disability in such a way that you can discuss it with others and educate them is critical to our society becoming more inclusive. Here are some further ideas:

■ Maintaining control over information that others have enables you to remain confident about your identity.

■ Presentation of your disability in a positive light assists with positive self-esteem.

■ The dispelling of assumptions and myths about your disability is critical in raising people's awareness of disability and makes it easier to have conversations as to how to address individual support requirements.

■ Allowing people to see you as an individual with strengths is critical as this is often overlooked. You are an individual with skills and a contribution to make to society, and as such this needs to be acknowledged.

Legislation

- Autism specific legislation (England). Autism is the only disability with specific legislation, and it emphasises the need to consult with autistic individuals and place them at the fore in conversations about the support they receive (Department of Health, 2010a; b; 2014).

- National Autism Strategy (Scotland), which is not legislation.

- Autism (Wales) Bill (2018).

- Autism Act (2011) Northern Ireland.

- The Republic of Ireland is also in the process of negotiating an Autism Bill.

- The Equality Act (2010). This assembles nine pieces of legislation pertaining to protected characteristics (age, disability, gender reassignment, race, religion or belief, sex and sexual orientation, marriage and civil partnership and pregnancy and maternity) asserting their equal value. This development accepts combined discrimination on the basis of two or more of these characteristics and embraces the diversity of identities to which individuals subscribe. It places a responsibility on the public sector to provide appropriate services accordingly.

- UN Convention on the Rights of Persons with Disabilities (EHRC, 2017). This is a human rights treaty ratified by the EU in 2010, which emphasises a need for autism awareness and protection of the rights of autistic individuals and accentuates training to address systemic failings and responsibilities. Furthermore, the UK government has committed itself to ensuring that these rights are fulfilled.

- Disability Support Allowance (DSA) and support. In order to obtain DSA at university in England, you need to provide GP/consultant evidence of your diagnosis/diagnoses. Support depends on individual needs as opposed to income. In Scotland, it is necessary to apply for a bursary or to go through the Student Awards Agency Scotland (SASS): http://www.saas.gov.uk/forms_and_guides/dsa.htm.

You can get help with the costs of:

- specialist equipment, for example a computer if you need one because of your disability

- non-medical helpers e.g. a mentor or notetaker

- extra travel because of your disability

- other disability-related costs of studying

- noise cancelling headphones

- tinted lenses.

You may get a new computer if you do not already have one, or your current one does not meet the required specification. You may have to make some contribution towards this depending on your circumstances. More information will be provided to you if you are assessed as needing a new computer: https://www.gov.uk/disabled-students-allowances-dsas/what-youll-get.

Employment

- The workplace is covered by the Equality Act (2010) and, if you disclose your disability/autism, reasonable adjustments should be discussed with you prior to interview and in the workplace.

- Equal opportunities forms will be separated from your application form by human resources, so the people interviewing you will not know about anything you state in this form.

- Being asked questions about health are not about ability to do the job, so you should NOT be asked anything that others are not asked.

Go to the Disability Rights UK website for more information:

https://www.disabilityrightsuk.org/telling-people-you%E2%80%99re-disabled-clear-and-easy-guide-students.

Concerns about disclosure

- Insider expertise not being acknowledged.

  - It is important to strike a balance between this and the university being able to discuss fairly with you what adjustments they could make to improve things so that you can study on an EQUAL basis to other students.

- Being judged unfairly.

  - If you have a support statement as a student, this should already take account of your support requirements.

  - In both the workplace and at university, the Equality Act (2010) is applicable and reasonable adjustments should be made if you have disclosed your disability.

- Others deciding your identity.
  This is why deciding who you disclose to is important, as it allows you to be who you are and express yourself in the way that you wish.

- Difficulty talking to a stranger about your disability.
  There is a difference between: empowered disclosure, where you feel comfortable with your identity; disclosing to chosen others and those with a responsibility to attend to your support requirements; and talking to a stranger about your disability, as you do not know how they will react. If you need to talk to a stranger about your disability (hospital staff, police etc), then take someone with you to support you.

Disability Rights UK student helpline

For further information on the support that is available for disabled students, please contact the disabled students helpline on 0800 328 50 50 (calls are free).

Tips for mentors and study skills support workers

- Disclosure is personal and brings several challenges as labels often mean that outsiders (people without that label or diagnosis) assume knowledge or that only one label is applicable.

- Discuss with students the importance of disclosure in certain contexts, but always on a need to know basis (unless they are confident and happy to disclose otherwise) to protect themselves.

- A disclosure plan should be established which addresses identity/identities, contexts, key people and why you might need to disclose e.g. to the emergency services or an employer.

- Also discuss situations where disclosure can make an individual more vulnerable e.g. in an environment where they have no support network or are experiencing bullying.

- Discuss legislation that impacts the student in this area to help support them in making a decision. However, do be realistic so that students are aware that disclosure does not always lead to equal treatment despite legislation.

Chapter 10: Focusing

Daydreaming

Daydreaming can often be a strategy used for:

- processing lots of information provided at the same time
- dealing with sensory overload
- dealing with anxiety and emotional overload.

In addition, many students find it incredibly difficult to focus their attention on the task in hand if they are not interested, and this can be more extreme among autistic students.

Too many questions

It can be quite difficult to process a number of questions asked in fairly quick succession, but this can be particularly challenging for autistic students as some may require longer to process information.

This is another area which is frequently misunderstood by staff and often mistaken as a student:

- Not understanding the question, so it then just gets repeated and the individual has to start processing it all over again, especially if it is not said in exactly the same way.

- Not wanting to answer. In this scenario, a student can be accused of not being willing to participate in course/group activities. This can cause a lot of distress to the student if time is not given. A mentor's input can be really helpful in assisting the student to explain what their exact difficulty is.

- Not knowing the answer. By not allowing an autistic student (or any student) time to process the question and formulate their answer, tutors would be robbing them of an opportunity to express their opinion. This is an extremely important aspect of learning for students at whatever level, so support and encouragement along with understanding will facilitate this process.

- Ignoring the person who asked the question. Any student who has asked a question, be it for clarification, to extend a debate, or whatever, should be encouraged to do so. If time has run out at the end of a lecture, details of where and when a tutor can be found are useful so that the individual can follow up on their question if they wish.

- Being confused. If students do not feel comfortable to ask for clarification, mentors or support workers can help. It may be that attending an individual tutorial takes pressure off the student, and they are then able to focus on the answer.

**One question at a time
...and wait for an answer**

Noise and distractions

Part of being a student is that you start to adapt to an adult learning style. This will help you fit into future work environments or patterns of working.

However, as keen as you may be to do this, there may be others who have not yet registered the importance of this and disrespect both the lecturers and other students. For this reason, it is good to:

- Arrive at the lecture well-prepared with the relevant learning materials.

- Arrive on time, as many lecturers will not let you into the lecture after 15 minutes have passed.

During the lecture, it is helpful not to:

- Speak to others while the lecturer is talking, as this can be distracting. If you don't understand something, you can check later or raise your hand to ask.

- Shuffle papers and your chair around as this is distracting and prevents others from hearing the lecturer.

The learning environment is talked about at different points in this book as it impacts on many people's ability to concentrate. Often the projector or lights are making a noise, which only those of us who are hyper sensitive can hear. This can be very distracting, so try to arrive early and find a quieter place in the room. You should have the handouts and accompanying information on your Learning Management System (LMS) e.g. Moodle or Canvas to help you.

Activity 10.1: Reflecting on learning

Some of the issues mentioned may apply to you, and it is important that you reflect on these either alone or with your mentor.

- You may find it useful to discuss these and think about situations in which they occur.

- Try to think of solutions to these, but it may take practise to change past habits, so don't be put off if they don't work immediately.

Activity 10.2: Being in the present moment

Try to calm or still your mind by focusing on your breath. You can do this in a lecture theatre or anywhere else. Just focus on bringing your breathing down so that your abdomen is rising and falling. Be aware of yourself sitting, and the contact your body is making with the chair. Notice the contact your feet are making with the floor. Breathe calmly.

Now start to focus on what is being said by the lecturer whilst maintaining this state of calm.

It may take time to practise this, but is definitely worth the effort (Black, 2012).

Focusing on coursework

This is dealt with in other chapters as it relates very much to the overall management of your work and how your mentor can help you (see Chapter 2 in particular).

Don't leave your least favourite subject till last. Rather do a small amount every day and you will soon have it completed. This way, it will not be too demanding on your ability to focus … many of us find this a challenge when we are less interested in something.

> Remember … a healthy balance between coursework and relaxation, combined with eating well and staying hydrated, will boost your ability to focus.

Tips for mentors and study skills support workers

- Help a student to prepare in advance for lectures and seminars e.g. by reading handouts, making notes, preparing possible questions.

- Discuss whether students are managing to process lecture/seminar information. Some may be able to listen and take notes at the same time, whereas others benefit from a voice recorder/note-taker. You may need to ask if they would like to request additional support through the disability advisor.

- Work with students to devise a plan to approach lecture/seminar material after the lecture e.g. reading notes, or highlighting material.

- Discuss the need for tutorials, either regularly or in response to a specific problem. Be prepared to attend to assist students in asking questions and processing answers if required. It may be that just setting up an initial meeting is all that is necessary to help build confidence.

- Identify with a student the best place for them to sit in different lecture theatres e.g. due to noise, movement from other students, lighting.

- Remind students of the strategies that they have at their disposal (and build up others) to assist them in dealing with large lecture rooms.

Chapter 11:
Wellness Recovery
Action Plan (WRAP)

Definition

Wellness Recovery Action Plan (WRAP) is a prevention and wellness process that is self-designed and can be used by anyone to become well and remain well. In addition, it allows you to put in place a recovery plan that suits you. As such, it is used by many people in a wide range of circumstances, and also by healthcare and mental health care practitioners. It can help you address physical and mental health as well as life issues.

A typical WRAP plan

A typical plan (Copeland, 2016) will enable you to:

- explore your own safe 'wellness tools'

- develop a list of daily activities to enable you to stay as well as possible

- identify upsetting events and early warning signs and indications that things have become worse or are becoming worse

- use wellness tools to develop action plans for helping you through these times

- assist you in the development of a crisis plan

- introduce you to post-crisis planning.

> **Remember... planning and forward thinking when you are well are key to maintaining well-being and critical in assisting a speedy recovery from illness.**

1. Exploring your own wellness tools

Resources that you may wish to put in this toolkit are surprisingly simple in theory, but much harder to engage in if we leave things until the last minute to do. So this is all about planning. The toolkit might include: contacting friends; using some activities to help you relax and to reduce your stress; writing a diary; affirmation activities; exercising; eating a healthy diet and having a good night's sleep. Also, changing the light in your room may help so that you use more natural light or daylight simulating light bulbs.

You may also find it helpful to keep a record of which activities worked best in which situations, and maybe others which you would like to try in the future.

2. Daily maintenance plan

This is a really important part of self-awareness as it is often difficult to describe how we are when we are feeling overwhelmed or really unwell.

Describe how you are when you feel well (you may wish to write this, list it, use a mind map, draw it). Note any mental or physical sensations. In addition to this, note what you do to maintain this state of well-being e.g. do you go out with friends, ask your mentor for help to engage with tricky aspects of your course, or do a sport?

3. Triggers

These are external events that cause us discomfort. It is quite normal for this to happen, but the reactions and discomfort needs to be dealt with somehow so that we do not feel worse or have a meltdown due to sensory/social overload.

4. Early warning signs

Early warning signs are critical in helping you to detect that things are not going well. At this stage, it is much easier for you to put an action plan in place and use your wellness toolkit.

These signs are often internal and subtle and let you know that you are beginning to feel worse. By reviewing these regularly, you will become familiar with them and act in a timely manner e.g. by deciding not to go out, but to stay in with a friend and do something quiet instead.

5. When things are breaking down

Writing down the signs that you are feeling worse is helpful for you, your mentor and your friends. These signs might be feeling sad all the time, feeling extremely anxious, or not sleeping.

At this point, you can use your wellness toolbox (ask your mentor or friends to help) to put together a powerful plan to help you feel well as quickly as possible before things become worse.

6. Crisis plan

You can work with your mentor to identify signs to alert others that they need to help you by taking responsibility for your care and decision making. By doing this at a time when you are feeling well, you are developing control over your well-being, and times of illness are not so distressing.

Your plan should include:

- Who you would like to have this responsibility.
- Healthcare – make a list of medications, doctors/consultants and any appointments.
- Taking pressure off you by informing tutors and asking your disability support worker to ask for extended deadlines for work if necessary.
- Ask your mentor to ask for coursework (notes) to be kept for you for when you are feeling well. This will help you not to worry.
- Note things that you do NOT want others to do as these would distress you further – it is often difficult to voice this when feeling unwell.

7. Post-crisis plan

This involves thinking about things you might need to address when you are feeling well again. For example, if you have been in hospital or have taken some time off to return home, what are the things that would be necessary to have in place to help you settle down as soon as possible?

You might want to:

- list these
- do a mind map
- draw a visual
- use a diary/planner.

When planning this, you may wish to include any thoughts about why each area mentioned is important as this might help you deal with any strong residual feelings.

Tips for mentors and study skills support workers

- The WRAP resource is great in that it allows you to work proactively with individual students to put a plan in place should they become unwell. I cannot emphasise the importance of this enough as feeling distressed and worrying about coursework demands can result in significant mental anguish. Therefore establishing a plan with your student(s) can be a real bonus and enable them to feel more confident about managing moments when they are feeling less productive or less engaged than at other times.

- The WRAP resource enables you to identify key people that students do or do not wish to be involved in their recovery, and at a time when they may be less able to voice this, having a plan written down is a real advantage.

- Encouraging students to reflect on positive activities, and which may not be too demanding, will be really critical if they become anxious or depressed, therefore build this into your activities early on.

- The WRAP facilitates the identification of both triggers and early warning signs such as physical, mental or emotional changes, and working with students on this aspect provides them with more understanding about and control over their lives. Again, begin discussing this as soon as your student feels comfortable talking with you and you can see that there is a level of trust being established between you.

- You can revisit this plan, and I would encourage you to do so from time to time as relationships and feelings change. This reminds the student that they have a plan there to be accessed if needs be and that it is also flexible. With some students, it may be necessary to address this in every session, in which case it can be established as a permanent part of the agenda.

- A post-crisis plan is as important as a WRAP plan as students may be distressed by events/feelings/or things said. Sensitivity is required to reassure and to adopt a strategy that enables them to feel in control once more.

Chapter 12: Intersectionality

We all have a range of identities and identity itself is a fluid concept. However, arguably one of the most disabling actions is that of labelling others. By placing them in a box, we impose boundaries and characteristics that may or may not be true, and restrict growth and self-expression in other co-existing identities.

Three students voice their different mentoring experiences of intersectionality as follows:

'When I first came out as transgender, my mentor was one of the only people who helped and supported me in that area. In my experience gender identity is not often talked about in relation to autism, despite the fact that there do exist quite a few autistic people who identify as trans. It is important to understand intersectionality because there are not separate "boxes" for each marginalised identity; often they can overlap.'

'When I started university I was extremely happy, however I came from a very strained situation concerning myself and family as well as previously being homeless. As a vulnerable autistic person from a black and minority ethic community (BAME), this was an extremely challenging and upsetting time for myself. I felt that my mentor supported me through this challenging time and is a key factor in why I am at university still, never allowing me to give up when I was ready to give up on myself.'

'Identifying as LGBTQ+ and having a disability has caused me to be discriminated against several times. Even though I may be privileged because I am white, I am still far from being within the majority. It is hard enough being in one minority but to be in two means you have to fight extra hard to be taken seriously.'

Some possible identities
Race, language, ethnicity, political ideology
Age, humanity, family and reproductive status
Gender, sexuality, habitat, mental health, class
Disability, citizenship, looks, skills, interests

Some key terms: (see Appendix 6)

These references give some key terms that are used today (Bornstein, 2013, Kenny *et al*, 2015) in relation to gender and autism. With both these and other identities there are too many to mention, so the best way to approach this with someone if you are unsure is to ASK.

Exploring intersectionality

The following activities encourage you to explore intersectionality in a reflexive way according to your communication preferences. You may wish to use a combination of these. Any of these activities might benefit from discussion with others in order to help you express things exactly as you wish. Essentially there is no wrong way of doing these activities. Their purpose is, among others:

1. To help you express yourself regarding your identity/identities.

2. To clarify some areas.

3. To compile a tool that might help others understand issues that are important to you, particularly if you are finding it difficult to explain these.

4. To have fun and relax.

Activity 12.1: How I want others to see me (mind map)

Consider which of the identities overleaf (or others) relate to you and are important for other people to know about. Do a mind map to include the following:

- What is it about each identity that is important to you?

- Why is this important?

- Think about past moments when people may have used this identity/these identities to discriminate against you?

- Think of the impact this had and write this down.

- What lessons can be learnt from this experience? Remember, it is possible to turn negative experiences into positive ones to move your life forwards.

- Write down a response to reflect why your identity is acceptable and should be respected by others (you may also want to discuss this with others who know you).

- Repeat this for any of the identities that are important to you, and you may want to add to this over time. Issues such as how we identify matter, as does voicing these in the way that we want.

- You may find that you want to change or add to some of the things that you have written as time passes, and that's quite typical as identity is a fluid phenomenon.

Activity 12.2: How I want others to see me (using a narrative diary to reflect)

For many, there is something appealing about using a narrative diary in that it permits and encourages the use of a wide array of materials e.g. photos, magazine/newspaper cut-outs, mixed media, sticking in mementos from past events such as a ticket or programme. The list continues, and it is up to the author to select things that work for them.

- Different sections of the diary can be used for different days or weeks, or to refer to different themes.

- You can return to themes at a later date to do them differently according to how you feel in the present moment. This is important as it shows you how you are processing information and developing as an individual, and is a great tool to share with someone to illustrate this point.

Try to use the diary regularly, especially if it assists you to think through difficulties that have arisen. An example of this may be if you are:

- autistic

- a trans man or woman

- experiencing gender dysphoria.

As feelings and difficult experiences happen, the narrative diary may help you work through these. This can be done separately and discussed with your mentor, or completed with your mentor.

Activity 12.3: How I want others to see me (using computer software to create a collage)

This is a repeat of Activity 12.2, but one that might appeal to those of you who are adept at using software packages such as Photoshop. Again, reflect on aspects of your identity that you want others to know about. These can then be expressed by selecting and manipulating images using Photoshop. You can create and update an array of designs, and this could even lead to a show of work.

Use your experiences creatively.

Tips for mentors and study skills support workers

- Intersectionality is an important theme to address throughout sessions with students, and I have found that it always arises under some guise or other. As students come to trust you, they may be more comfortable discussing this issue with you as it does tackle the two related themes of labelling/terminology and disclosure.

- Some students may not be familiar (and you may not be either!) with different terms relating to intersectionality, so this is a good starting point for a conversation. Some terms are written in Appendix 6, and these might facilitate discussion e.g. are they relevant or useful to your particular student? Do they agree with this language?

- There is immense power in being able to use the language, terminology and identities that we wish to, so provide your students with as much opportunity to do this as possible. My experience is that initial caution is eventually overcome, often quite quickly, only to taken over by a sense of relief that there is a forum for addressing this topic.

- Support students in discussing how they can turn bad experiences around and use them as good ones. This helps tackle issues of anxiety, avoidance, anger and fear, and is critical for the student's well-being.

- Discussing good and bad experiences can provide an enormous sense of release to students, and particularly when they know that they are not on their own. Perhaps introduce the idea that they may like you to introduce them to others with similar experiences – you could establish a debating/discussion group.

- Narrative diaries are an excellent tool for students going through experiences such as cultural changes or gender dysphoria. Encourage the student to begin a scrapbook type of diary and include writing, photos, drawings, magazine cut-outs or whatever material which helped or hindered their identity development. Reflection on this can be included in part of the support session if the student wishes, or in the latter example, it may help them talk to a gender specialist and voice their thoughts and feelings.

Chapter 13: Gender

As an autistic student, unless you have requested a mentor for mental health support, you will have been signposted to a mentor for autism-related support or support with well-being, and you can also access on-campus academic support accordingly. You can also have support if you have documentary evidence that you are gender non-binary or trans, or are transitioning and require support with mental well-being, though it may be more difficult to do so (SFE, 2018).

The challenges impacting on well-being for many autistic students who are exploring their gender or sexuality positively, often go unacknowledged. This section endeavours to address some of the issues raised by students.

> **Remember...your view of gender is what matters.**

Identity and well-being

Students who do not identify as cisgender (with a sense of personal identity and gender corresponding with their birth sex), but who may identify as gender non-binary or genderqueer (being on a spectrum of gender identities that are not exclusively masculine or feminine) or transgender, may be provided with a mentor who only understands the autism side of their identity. Clearly this can be problematic as you may feel that you wish to discuss issues in this area.

This systemic failure to acknowledge additional identities within an individual can impact on how you initially feel you can relate to your mentor, but they are there to work with you holistically.

> **Remember...identities overlap.**

Coming out

This is likely to be a lifelong journey where you explore your identity. In other words, it is about understanding, accepting and acknowledging your identity and what it means to you before you can express this readily and confidently to others. So coming out has to be at a time that suits you.

Activity 13.1: Looking at points you wish to address

This activity is critical to helping you to explore your identity and your agenda for coming out (also see Chapter 5, Activity 5.4). Take two pieces of paper, and on one draw the outline of a generic body i.e. head, torso, arms and legs with nothing else marked, and on the second, divide it with a cross from top to bottom and left to right.

- On the first sheet, annotate the diagram in terms of feelings, emotions and issues important to you in relation to selected body parts/areas and how these impact on you now.
- On the second sheet, mark the squares as follows:
  - Feelings that you hope to have (top left square).
  - Emotions that you would like to experience more (top right square).
  - Changes that you would like to see in your life as a result of coming out (bottom right square).
  - Hopes in terms of people who you would like to accept you (bottom left square).
- As you finish the second part of this activity, you should be able to see a development in terms of your identity

Remember...accept yourself and take time to explore who you are and want to be. You are valuable.

There is no right way or right time to come out, and many young people do this at college. At this life stage, identity is often being explored. There are lots of resources to support you.

Further activities in Chapters, 9 (disclosure), 12 (intersectionality) and 16 (self-esteem and confidence-building) will also be helpful.

Understanding pronouns

You may already have decided on the use of different pronouns to express your identity. For example, you may put she/her and they/them after your name to indicate those that are acceptable to you. Also, you may experiment with pronouns to reflect your changing identity, so reminding others of what you are comfortable with is important. There are many pronouns to choose from and websites to explore (see Chapter 22).

Autism and Mental Well-being in Higher Education © Pavilion Publishing and Media Ltd and its licensors 2020. **103**

Gender neutral/gender inclusive pronouns

This type of pronoun does not link a gender with a specific person. The English language does not have a gender neutral pronoun like many other languages (e.g. German) so many people will explore different pronouns in order to avoid the dichotomous she/he.

- It is important to avoid the use of 'it' or 'he-she' when referring to someone who is trans or gender non-conforming as these are offensive terms.

There are many gender neutral pronouns in use such as:

- Just using a person's name and no pronoun.
- Ze (pronounced zee)/hir/zir e.g. Charlie took some photos because ze wanted to inform hir portfolio.
- They/them/theirs e.g. George attends their University because they want to be a costume designer.

Mis-gendering

Remember, people do make mistakes, and educating others in this area is key to informing inclusion. People can be awkward if a mistake has been made about their identity or if they make a mistake about someone else's. So there are two key points to consider here which can assist:

- Having someone misgender you.

Although this can be hurtful, remind the other person of your preferred pronoun (or ask your mentor or someone else to do this for you) and explain the importance of this.

- Misgendering others.

Understanding and using an individual's preferred pronouns is important and respectful to them. If you make a mistake, apologise either immediately, or if you notice later, you could apologise privately.

If you have changed the pronouns you are more comfortable using to reflect your gender change, be patient with others and use gentle reminders as soon as possible so that your new identity is understood.

Maybe use a pronoun badge or add preferred pronouns to the bottom of an email, as is increasingly popular.

Understanding name change

■ Informal name changes.

Saying something such as 'I prefer to be known as ... now' can inform your peers, tutors, disability advisor and mentor accordingly.

■ Formal name changes can be divided into three distinct areas:

   ■ First, where you have come out or are in the process of coming out as having a different gender identity. You may wish to change your name on your university ID to help avoid feelings of gender dysphoria and to feel validated. Many university systems have not managed to address this efficiently yet. You can ask your students' union for support and your mentor/disability advisor may be able to liaise with people either with you or on your behalf.

   ■ Second, changing your name on the university system, and particularly in respect of the name on your degree certificate, needs to be recognised. Check whether the university system will address this is in place and if not, your disability advisor, mentor and the students' union should be able to help.

   ■ Changing your name by deed poll is a simple three-step process. Hurray! There are several processes, but the official online process is the cheapest.

   Apart from changing your name formally on university documents, it will allow you to change your name on your passport, driving licence and on bank cards. This is important as they are all formal and acceptable forms of ID. You are provided with a list of people who you should advise of a name change and a letter template to do so.

   The official deed poll site is: https://www.ukdeedpolloffice.org/how-do-i-change-my-name/?msclkid=37eb95b3a2a619a4a8a6c88fea4fc2a4&utm_source=bing&utm_medium=cpc&utm_campaign=Deed%20Poll&utm_term=%2Bdeed%20%2Bpoll%20%2Bchange&utm_content=Deed%20Poll%20Change%20Name

Under equality legislation, it can be argued that universities need to recognise names when you are in transition. The Diversity and Inclusion Officer at your university can advise.

Transitioning

The process of transitioning is complex and unique. The route in the UK is to discuss this with your GP and ask them to refer you to a gender specialist. However, the list may be lengthy depending on where you are in the country.

A disadvantage of waiting is counteracting feelings of dysphoria, but an advantage can be that you have more time to explore aspects of the process, questions you may want answered and so on. There is support both with this aspect within and outside your university (see Chapter 22).

Working with support staff to understand transitioning

Unless you have asked the disability advisor to disclose your gender identity, this information will generally NOT have been passed to your mentor.

An exception to this will be if you have asked for support with your well-being.

You can choose to let your mentor know about your gender and whether you wish to discuss the impact of this aspect of your identity with them. More importantly, if it is impacting on your well-being you may wish to request more focused support:

- outside the university e.g. through LGBTQ+ centres
- inside the university e.g. through the wellbeing team, or
- whether you would liked to be signposted to one of these options.

If you wish to discuss gender identity with your mentor, they should support you to identify your agenda i.e. what is impacting on your well-being and your studies? (See Appendix 7: Setting your agenda).

Remember...your mentor is there to support you in understanding the intersections of your identity.

Activity 13.2: Identifying and exploring resources

- Explore different websites and resources.
- Identify areas for discussion.
- Use this to inform and address your support needs i.e.

Activity 13.3: Identifying groups

It is helpful to identify groups:

- within the university
- outside the university.

These both provide opportunities for you to build friendships and networks and have conversations with peers. This is invaluable in helping you to identify as you wish and also to find new groups to join.

In addition, you are always free to set up your own group within the university if you would like. Talk to the students' union, your disability advisor or your mentor about this.

Discrimination and inclusion

Inappropriate comments and unnecessary requests for information are both hurtful and unacceptable. These can be dealt with by talking to:

- your disability advisor

- your mentor

- your students' union LGBTQ+ officer

- your university's Diversity and Inclusion Officer.

If the comments have been made intentionally and maliciously, they are covered by both equality and hate crime legislation and also by university policies. The university should take a very strong view with immediate action.

**Remember...discrimination
and hate crime are illegal and
your university should act
immediately to support victims.**

Relationships

Coming out, transitioning and developing relationships can be enormously complex.

- If you are already in a relationship and decide to transition, this may then impact on the gender identity of your partner, and you may both wish to have support talking through the implications of this.

- If you have had an intimate relationship with someone and then felt that you wished to explore/express your gender differently, this may bring you mixed and unexpected feelings. Again, there is support (see Chapter 22).

- If you have had no prior intimate relationships and want support to discuss your gender identity and sexual orientation, sexual health clinics can provide specialist support.

There are many other issues arising under this heading, and the reading list at the end of this book provides useful suggestions to inform you.

Gender inclusive restrooms (toilet facilities) on campus

These should be marked on the university map. If not, have a word with the students' union as one of their roles is to campaign for the rights of students at the university.

Tips for mentors and study skills support workers

- If you hear one of your mentees being misgendered, or they report this to you, you could ask if they would like support addressing this by reminding the other person of the pronouns to use and why this is important.

- If you do not know which pronouns to use, ask. A failure to do this can leave your mentee feeling invalidated, dysphoric, alienated and disrespected.

- It is important that the experiences of any mentee coming out are validated, especially for those in transition, as they may be experiencing increased feelings of not being in control of their bodies or how people see them. An approach that acknowledges this facilitates control.

- If you are not familiar with transitioning, try to inform yourself generally, but remember that each insider experience is unique. Sensitive listening and appropriate questions are key to building trust and helping the mentee become more confident in talking to you or seeking specialist support.

- If your mentee discloses discrimination or hate crime, reassure them that you are taking this seriously, discuss their options with them and support them.

- Encourage your mentee to explore different groups and activities to combat feelings of isolation.

Chapter 14:
BAME (black and minority ethnic communities)

Many BAME children and adults struggle to obtain or accept an autism diagnosis for additional reasons to those from other societal sectors. This can be influenced by delays due to family and cultural traditions, religious beliefs and language barriers. There may also be difficulties experienced in obtaining support at a family or community level or within the education system, and for these reasons, this area has always been problematic for BAME communities.

BAME communities and communication

Conversations with individuals from BAME communities have highlighted very different approaches to autism imposed by family, ranging from:

- Acceptance.
- Denial
- Embarrassment.
- Seeing a family member as gifted or special and not meriting support.
- Discipline which does not show an understanding of the support required by the individual.
- Sending an autistic family member back to the parents'/the individual's country of origin in the hope that the culture and disciplinary approaches there will better meet the individual's needs. Clearly this can be distressing for an individual in relation to a number of aspects of autism, for example, change, sensory and social overload, communication.

Diagnosis

This factor often impacts negatively on BAME autistic students at all educational levels, and is frequently voiced as an institutional failure to understand them. This promotes and exacerbates discrimination and can manifest itself in the more frequent use of labels such as 'aggressive' to explain an individual's personality, as opposed to recognising distress or a response to matters such as change or sensory and social overload.

As a student at university, if you have a diagnosis of autism you are entitled to disability support. If you do not have a diagnosis of autism, a disability or recognition of a mental health problem you are entitled to ask for an assessment. You can go to:

- your GP for support, advice and help
- the Disability Support Services on university campus

- specialist services for local advice and support groups.

The advantages of this are that:

- You can receive support which includes both equipment and also a specialist mentor.
- You can have flexibility around deadlines for academic work. This allows time for additional processing, reading and structuring of work.

As a student in HE, you may experience challenges and barriers due to your individual and overlapping identities, namely:

- being from a BAME community
- being autistic
- any other identity
- intersections of these identities.

Activity 14.1: Prior to a diagnosis

If you have requested a diagnosis, or are thinking of doing so, you may find it useful to list or map areas of difficulty for you. This may be easier to do with a family member or friend as they can prompt you with questions or comments about shared environments e.g. school. Think about what is easy or difficult about any of the following:

- Communication e.g. what are your communication preferences?
- Environments that are more enabling for you e.g. where you can learn or relax.
- Friendships or social activities e.g. do you have any difficulties or preferences in this area?
- Sensory experiences i.e. are you hyper- or hypo-sensitive to anything? If so, what?

Having done this, you can share this information with the diagnostician(s) if you wish as it will be useful in informing the process.

Activity 14.2: Mapping challenges and barriers

Poor school experiences often impact widely on autistic individuals, but the double discrimination faced by those from BAME communities results in higher rates of exclusions than experienced by their white peers. If this has been your experience, you may wish to address this in one of your mentoring sessions as the impact of it may carry forward into your expectations of higher education.

Either on your own, or with someone who you are comfortable with, e.g. your mentor, take a sheet of paper and:

- Map the areas of difficulty that you have faced prior to university in terms of learning and friendships, expressing your voice and being heard (this is useful in terms of understanding how you have managed to tackle these, if you have).

- On a separate sheet of paper, map the current challenges and barriers you are experiencing in relation to the same areas and your whole university experience i.e. learning, social life, accommodation.

This should give you and your mentor plenty of material to discuss in terms of areas that are important for you to address.

Activity 14.3: Discussing what constitutes an enabling environment for you

Using the information from the above activity, discuss with your mentor some possible strategies and solutions to combat your barriers. These should enable you to learn and perform at your best. You may wish to share some of this information with:

- tutors
- the head of year/course

You can then put these in your toolbox for future reference. As barriers have a habit of repeating themselves and transitioning between contexts, practice your solutions and responses to build confidence and familiarity with these.

Representation of BAME voices within HE and other services

There is a lack of representation of BAME autistic people or those with autistic family members at staff or organisational levels, and in particular within Disability Support Services across universities. This can also mean that the above issues impacting on BAME communities, in addition to intersectionality and a need for a similar peer group, go misunderstood. Communication with white authority figures within an elitist system can result in exclusion from meaningful conversations and a tokenistic approach by staff.

Activity 14.4: Exploring inclusion, exclusion and tokenism

Discuss, list and map out key points regarding inclusion and tokenism in respect of your identity and your journey at all stages of the university process, i.e:

- application

- interview and accommodations

- acceptance.

Look at how this impacts on you now. Put some strategies in place to deal with these stages at later points i.e. another university level or employment.

Individuals from BAME communities do access services outside the HE environment, but the documentation of this is often poor and results in their numbers being inaccurately recorded. This may be through a number of channels, for example official documentation, questionnaires and surveys. Clearly this may then impact on the numbers of BAME mentors (and SEN teachers within earlier education) with whom autistic BAME students may better identify.

> Remember ... each level of education brings different experiences and opportunities.

Isolation

This is often an experience of autistic students, and those from BAME communities may experience it in relation to both identities.

Activity 14.5: Setting up an inclusive group

Think about what specific support needs you have on a social level. If there are no BAME groups that address your needs within your university, you could think about setting one up.

- Talk about this with your mentor.

- Map out or list ideas on paper.

- Think about the purpose of the group e.g. for autistic BAME students to meet and discuss issues; to raise awareness of the needs of autistic BAME students within your university.

- Think about how often it would meet e.g. weekly, fortnightly, monthly.

- Think about where and when the group could meet e.g. in a social space on or off campus e.g. book a room on campus, or meet in a cafe; off campus you may like to meet in a quiet cafe or bar.

- Who else could help you establish the group and publicise it? For example, think about asking the students' union or your Disability Support Worker, or another student(s).

BAME organisations

In the UK, there are a number of BAME organisations, but one which specifically focuses on the HE environment among other issues is called Autism Voice UK (AUVoice UK). It is based at London South Bank University and operates under the umbrella of the Participatory Autism Research Collective (see Chapter 22). Its founder, Mariama Kandeh, has campaigned successfully to encourage members of the BAME community to access the MA Autism course at London Southbank University. This is in order that the UK sees more BAME practitioners and researchers in this field.

AUVoice UK held its first symposium in early 2019 to address and inform areas of interest and concern to this community. Its success demonstrates a need to repeat the event, and further information about the organisation can be found in Chapter 22.

Addressing the agenda of BAME individuals should be central to their mentoring and inclusion within HE. Discrimination and bullying may be experienced by individuals.

Tips for mentors and study skills support workers

- If you are a mentor who is NOT from the BAME community, check what the agenda is for the student(s)

- you are mentoring. It is important to fully understand the intersection of their identities in order to provide support.

- An awareness of issues relating to BAME communities and also intersectionality is helpful as it can inform discussions.

- Be aware of a need to discuss safe spaces with students who feel threatened, discriminated against or who may be victim-survivors of hate crime.

- Work with students to see how invaluable and enriching diverse communities and multiculturalism are to student life. Use this to build confidence in individuals and link with student union activities.

Chapter 15:
Sexual violence and available support on and off campus

**Remember...sexual violence
occurs among all ages, genders,
sexual orientations, disabilities,
ethnicities or faith groups
and their intersections.**

Legislation and understanding of sexual violence

Definition of sexual violence is covered by The Sexual Offences Act (2003) c.42, and this also details changes in legislation. The act covers sexual violence by an acquaintance (i.e. a known individual) or an unknown individual(s), and whether the incident occurred on a single or multiple occasions. The key areas covered by this legislation are:

- rape
- sexual assault
- sexual abuse
- child and sexual exploitation (CSE)
- consent.

**Remember...no means no – but just
because somebody hasn't said 'no'
doesn't mean they mean 'yes'.**

Sexual violence on and off campus

Incidents of sexual violence may occur at any time (or not at all). For example, they may occur prior to you coming to university or whilst at university.

Support relating to reporting/accessing well-being support will relate to your current life, and so you can request this from university services, health or specialist services, the criminal justice system or a mixture of these.

There may be a number of different influences impacting on the choice you make, including:

- You may not wish to report the incident(s) formally, but do wish to access well-being support.

- If you are a victim-survivor of historical rape prior to coming to university and have not disclosed, support systems are in place to help you both within and outside university, should you wish to explore your options. For example, these may be formal reporting to the police, accessing specialist support or accessing student well-being support.

- You may have experienced sexual violence prior to university and be in the process of disclosing it formally to police.

- You may have disclosed to the police and be accessing support from specialist services e.g. The Survivors' Trust, the Rape and Sexual Violence Project or Women's Aid.

- You may have already disclosed to the police and be accessing support from mental health services.

- Student well-being services may be supporting you.

Your university should have a policy in respect of sexual violence on campus, in relation to both peers and staff and addressing issues relating to intersectionality. Your disability advisor or student support service can inform you as to the relevant procedures.

Shamefully, there remains huge inconsistency in policy development and implementation in this area. However, it is important to know you have a right to feel safe whilst studying and accessing all areas in and around the university, and you may wish to raise any areas of concern with the students' union.

Reporting sexual violence

Reporting sexual violence is not easy for survivors. Yet its current high prevalence both on and off campus makes it an issue that merits attention.

Societal responses also demonstrate a need for those on the receiving end of disclosures to be aware of issues, to be confident of providing appropriate and validating responses, and for those in positions of authority there needs to be an understanding of safeguarding issues and reporting protocol.

Importantly, victim-survivors should be aware of the following:

- It is not essential to report to the police.

- It is important to access health support as soon as possible as you are at risk of sexually transmitted infections (STIs).

- You may be at risk of pregnancy.

Activity 15.1: Processing and communicating the incident

Trauma has a massive impact on the memory, and this affects individuals uniquely. It may be that you recall bits of information at different times, so it is important to access one of your tools built up throughout this book to allow you to do this.

In addition to this, you may find it easier to process your thoughts using your preferred communication format. This may make things easier for you regardless of whether you choose to report the incident formally/access well-being support, or both.

Chapter 8 of this book introduced you to some different ways of communicating that you may wish to try, and it is important that you choose what suits you. Nevertheless, something that would allow you to incorporate the following may well prove to be useful:

- Timeline of events.
- Emotions diary.
- Enabling and disabling environments.

Disclosure and support

The purpose of this chapter is to provide an overview of options so that you can take more specialist advice. For this reason, guidance is provided to the main routes where you can then access this specialist advice. This is in addition to support staff in student services, where you disclose to your disability worker, mentor or the well-being team.

There are three main access points for formal support if you are a victim-survivor of sexual violence:

- The more formal approach is to report to the police, and they can discuss processes with you.
- Help can be obtained through a Sexual Assault Referral Centre (SARC), these are specialist services including The Survivor's Trust, the Rape and Sexual Violence Project (RSVP), Women's Aid and NHS referral centres. They can support you with all parts of the process e.g. accessing a forensic medical examination, providing support to speak to the police, exploring and informing you about all aspects of the court process, including the support from an Independent Sexual Violence Advocate (ISVA). You can self-refer to a SARC (go to google and add 'SARC + your area'). Their approach is completely person-centred.

- You can ask your GP to be signposted to counselling, psychological therapies or mental health support. The choice is yours.

Sexual violence is about someone imposing power over you and taking away control, so part of your recovery journey may be about regaining control in a manner that suits you and at a pace that allows for the processing of information. Think about the model of support you would like.

- Does it involve talking?

- Does it involve taking medication?

- Is it a combination of these?

With each service, it may be a good idea to check the waiting list as this may influence your choice. In addition, it will help if you are aware of the range of support available, for example: GPs, counsellors, psychologists and psychotherapists. Endeavour to be informed so that you remain in control of your support as much as possible and can recover your well-being in the best way for you.

Whilst you may choose/be able to disclose to friends and family due to a supportive network, there are other options.

- Your disability advisor has a safeguarding duty and can support you in accessing appropriate services either on or off campus.

- Your tutor/head of department equally has a safeguarding duty, and can liaise with your disability advisor to help you access the support you wish.

- If you have a mentor, they can help you to disclose the incident to your disability advisor and can signpost you to other services. They do, however, have a duty to report the incident to your disability advisor in order that the university can perform its safeguarding responsibilities.

- Specialist Services are able to support you off campus in the event that you wish to separate out the incident from university life. In addition, as their name suggests, they can provide specialist information and support regarding health support, counselling and all aspects of the report to court process among other things.

- Your GP can signpost you to mental health support, for example psychological services and specialist services among others.

**Remember...you do have choices
around your recovery support.**

Pregnancy following rape

Pregnancies can and do sometimes follow rape, and if you find yourself in this situation, it is important to remember that help and support is there and that you do have choices. You can access any of the support mentioned previously for further.

Chapter 7 provides several activities for managing anxiety and stress, which will be really helpful for you at this time. Keep practising them.

> **Remember...rape is NOT your fault.
> Support IS there.**

Sex education and support

Whilst this should be embedded in education systems at all levels, there is evidence that many disabled and autistic individuals have little or no access to sex education. However, it is never too late to educate yourself.

Leaflets and booklets can be obtained through NHS Foundation Trusts or through sexual health services. An example of the latter is Umbrella, which is part of University Hospital Birmingham NHS Foundation Trust. This service covers issues such as STIs, contraception, advice for gay men, advice for young people, pregnancy advice and support and the services are confidential.

Sex education should teach the rudimentaries of body parts and what role they play in terms of having good sex or procreation. It should incorporate discussions which build on knowledge gathered to support young people to grow into healthy adults. If you are a more mature adult, this information can be adapted to suit your needs.

Good sex education should also dispel myths. For example, when you can and can't become pregnant, or what constitutes consent in terms of having any sex.

Intimate relationships

> **Remember...good sex is consensual
> sex enjoyed by both parties.**

Peer pressure often plays a big role in young people choosing to have sexual relationships, with a variety of outcomes. Regardless of your reason, it is critical to be aware that your body is yours and that nobody else has a right to impose anything on it without your consent.

The ONLY exceptions to this would be:

- If you were at risk of harming yourself.
- If you were at risk of harming others.

Coercive relationships are those where you find yourself living under constant threats and judgements by a partner. For example, they may constantly question your clothing, or where you go, or who you talk to. This behaviour is usually underpinned by a deep sense of insecurity and jealousy, among other things, and you may well wish to access support from sexual health or well-being services to discuss your options.

Tips for mentors and study skills support workers

- Be familiar with safeguarding policy and practice within your university.
- Familiarise yourself with available support both within and outside the university.
- Get to know your student so that you can be aware of any changes in their behaviour e.g. irritability, lack of ability to focus, over-dependency on some people and a need to avoid others.
- Be aware of things that may be triggering e.g. crowded environments, noisy spaces, a lot of people bumping into and touching your mentee unexpectedly.
- Get to know your students' tutors so that you can raise any concerns with them e.g. are academic targets being met? How is their overall attendance? What about their ability to build friendships/be involved in group work?
- Encourage discussion around avoidance of people or places.
- Recognise that in disclosing, a student is taking the first and bravest step in managing the sexual violence to which they have been subjected.
- Be aware that your mentee may prefer to access support outside the university, as managing sexual violence whilst studying may be overwhelming.
- Look at available options for your mentee and discuss these with the disability advisor and the mentee e.g. taking a year out.

Chapter 16: Self-esteem and confidence-building

Students develop a range of ways to build their self-esteem and develop their confidence in a new environment and according to their identities. The following chapter includes a range of activities that you may find helpful to explore alone or with your mentor.

'A most recent example for me is applying for my job at the students' union. In order to get it I had to be voted in. The thought of this terrified me, I didn't think people would like me enough to vote for me and I didn't think I could do a job involving helping students so soon after finishing university. I realised that I had to at least try because I owed it to myself and to other students. I now know that confidence and self-esteem is an ongoing process, but you always have to challenge yourself and constantly tell yourself you can do it, because you are your biggest supporter, if you believe in you, then others will, and then from this self-belief you can achieve great things and make positive change.'

Positive self-talk

Activity 16.1: Positive mantras and where to leave them

Sometimes it is difficult to think positively, so a good activity is to build up a collection of mantras.

> **Look for positive mantras and sayings in books and on post-it notes around your house or room or on the internet. Post them on sticky notes on your computer screen so that you will see them as soon as the computer comes on.**

Activity 16.2: Post-it notes (for any day)

Whilst we do not need an excuse to leave positive messages for ourselves or each other, I have frequently come across a batch of notes and a pen left for people to fill in and stick to a surface for others to enjoy. More recently, on International Women's Day, I came across a pile of blank post-it notes and a pen in the women's toilet at the university where I was working. Women had already begun to fill these in with positive affirmations and stick them on the mirror. Themes addressed were around:

- survival

- recovery

- well-being

- being strong

- being valued

- being loved

- loving and caring for someone.

All themes have touched me and left me with the feeling that, no matter who we are, or what is going on in our lives at any one moment, these affirmations are a good thing. Positive messages tap into the healthy chemicals in the brain and give us a feel-good factor. The great news is that we can do this any time and regardless of who we are, or where we are, although sharing them is brilliant.

Evidence demonstrates that negative thoughts and feelings about life's events encourage feelings of stress, depression and illness. Positive thinkers, on the other hand, send warm vibes to others and can cope with life better. So this type of activity might well work for you.

Activity 16.3: Positivity journal

Developing a positivity journal can really help you flick the switch and focus on what is going right in your life. This is really important at times when negative life events seem to be taking over, and it allows us to maintain a grip on the good things happening in our lives.

Try to add three things at the end of each day. They do not have to be complicated.

Items to include may be around:

- activities such as meditation or a sport

- planning or structuring an assignment

- cooking

- tidying your room

- talking to a friend.

The more often you engage in this activity, the easier it will become for you to focus on the positives in your life.

Tips for mentors and study skills support workers

- Work with your students to explore their barriers to self-confidence and self-esteem. Once you have a good idea of these, together you can look at a plan to address them e.g. joining an activity group; being able to disclose their identity in the way they wish; being able to come out.

- Encourage your student to build up a collection of positive mantras. A new one each week is a good starting point. Then putting it somewhere visible where it will be remembered and repeated is a good routine to encourage.

- Encourage any student that you are working with who is struggling with depression or low self-esteem to start to work on a positivity journal. This is a really useful way to assist them in focusing and reflecting on the parts of their day/week/life that are working, as it will be difficult for them to appreciate this at the low moments. Initially you may want to do this activity together to start it off and review it, and talking about the good aspects, however little, can be a great boost to a student's confidence.

Part 3:
Being independent

Chapter 17: Independent living

Student accommodation

As a student you have a range of accommodation options available, and everybody has their own preferences. Things you might want to consider:

- Sensory concerns such as closeness to a busy road.

- Proximity to your campus (look at the area at night, so you get a sense of how safe you feel in the area).

- Ease of navigation between your accommodation and the university.

- Lighting. Check that the lighting around the area you will live in gives you the sense that you would feel safe returning there later in the evening in the dark.

- Whether there is good local public transport.

- Whether you will be sharing with others.

- Whether you have you own bathroom.

- Who you will be sharing with.

Activity 17.1: Decorating my room

If in student accommodation, there are rules that you will be given about fixing things, such as posters, to walls. It is useful to use the notice board to display:

- Timetables.

- Current timetable and deadlines.

- A calendar including the above two things.

How about adding a plant? It doesn't have to be big, and ones such as cacti only need a little care as they look after themselves really well. Green plants are peaceful, for instance yucca plants.

Activity 17.2: Knowing your flatmates

Who do you share with? Your flatmates will probably be keen to know you too, and it is good to find out if you have things in common with them such as interests, places where you went to school/FE or the course you are studying. Try this activity to get to know your flatmates better:

- Each of you could draw a shield with four sections and a motto.

- Section one is something you like to eat.

- Section two is something you would like to do with others at university.

- Section three is something you like to do alone.

- Section four might be somewhere you have travelled to and found interesting.

- Finally, think of a motto that expresses who you are – this could be serious or funny.

Activity 17.3: Identifying relevant staff to deal with difficult situations and build coping strategies

Some situations at university may arise where you may encounter difficulties and need a strategy in place. The following is a useful template from which to work, and details can be added with your mentor according to the situation(s) experienced:

- Talk about the problem with the relevant people if you can e.g. if you are experiencing difficulties with flatmates, such as noise, they may not be aware of this, and a simple request to turn the noise level down may work.

- Talk to your mentor and put some ideas together to resolve the problem.

- Talk to the relevant staff members e.g. the accommodation officer if the problem concerns your accommodation, or a finance officer if you have financial difficulties.

- Talk to the disability support worker as they will have a broad range of contacts throughout the university.

- Talk to security services at the university e.g. if you are being threatened or harassed.

Activity 17.4: Buying cookbooks and learning to cook

Can you cook? If so that's great, as it can also help with independent living and building friendships. If not, now is a really great opportunity for you to learn, and with so many books on the shelves and recipes on the internet you have lots of choice. These will teach you:

- what cooking equipment is needed

- different cooking methods e.g. frying, roasting, baking

- how to use certain kitchen equipment

- what ingredients are needed

- how to prepare the meals themselves.

You may take a while to practise certain recipes, but don't worry … many top chefs talk about learning best from their mistakes!

> **Pay attention to what you are doing, the colours and smell of the ingredients such as the vegetables, fruits and herbs, rather than seeing them as things you don't like. The possibility of creating a tasty meal then becomes more plausible.**

Once you have some recipes (or even just one) that you like, you can invite someone round for dinner. It's cheaper than eating out and if you find social events challenging it gives you a chance to get to know someone with whom you have something in common on a one-to-one basis.

You may have avoided cooking due to sensory sensitivities in relation to smells and textures, but remember, you have control over this and can choose the food you want to buy and prepare.

Activity 17.5: Familiarising yourself with local area/bus route(s)

Getting to know a new area can be a little daunting for some of us, although others are excited by this prospect. Either way, it's a good idea to familiarise yourself with your environment. This will help you to feel more settled into university life and the wider social and possible course tasks, which may require you to visit certain areas of the city or locality.

- Find someone to explore town with you.
- Ask your mentor to help you.
- Ask your course tutor to help you.

Activity 17.6: Shopping

Going to the shops at quieter times may be less stressful for you; perhaps in the evening or on a Sunday. Planning is also helpful, so you could think about what you would like to eat over the week and then write a list of ingredients.

In my experience shops can be daunting for a range of reasons, although some people may not find this the case. Among these reasons are:

- Lighting (too bright or too dim).

- Sound (lots of different noises going on at the same time).

- Shopping malls/centres (the echo and social overload can be extreme).

- Busy places (sensory overload as lots of people bump into you).

- Smells (items such as perfumes or cleaning fluids can trigger strong reactions).

- Noise from air conditioners or lighting.

- Social anxiety can take the enjoyment out of the activity.

Coping strategies:

Wear tinted glasses or make a note of shops with good lighting.

Go to the shops at quieter times (early or later in the day).

Going to social events, conventions and conferences

Different social events, conventions and conferences can be fun. However, if you are someone who experiences sensory sensitivities or social anxiety, it is definitely a good idea to go to these with some coping strategies in place.

Social events

If you naturally prefer quieter spaces, there are many around. You may want to identify these with a friend or your mentor, or a tutor as well if these are related to your course.

Alternatively, experimenting with different venues might appeal to you as long as you are with someone/a group of friends you feel safe with.

- Make sure you have a coping strategy in place if a social situation becomes difficult for you and you become anxious.

- If you have a friend you trust, make sure that they know how to support you best in this situation, whilst giving you the space to be in as much control as possible.

Conventions and conferences

Remember ... you are your own best friend and expert. Notice when you are beginning to feel stressed, and calmly remove yourself from the situation and go to a quieter area.

There are many non-autistic people who are aware about the need to make reasonable adjustments at conferences. Due to the increasing number of autistic speakers, a quiet area is now often requested by both speakers and organisers.

If you need a quiet area, ask, or someone can request this for you. Reasonable adjustment is a legal responsibility.

Tips for mentors and study skills support workers

■ The whole student experience is critical to people's success at university, and for those who are living in student accommodation (halls or otherwise), this experience brings many often-unexpected challenges. Familiarise yourself with these as much as possible so that you can introduce conversations around these in the early stages. If your student is aware that you are familiar with these areas, they may be more comfortable to discuss them with you should problems arise.

■ Sensory concerns can be really stressful for students, so ensure that you address these regularly.

■ Safety is another worry for individual students, so check that they have a plan, a contact number, and an autism card should they wish. In addition, they may wish to do some self-defence classes.

■ Help students build relationships with their flatmates early on as this will help should disagreements occur at a later stage. Also discuss what to do if there are recurring issues, such as noise or lack of respect for personal space.

- Discussing shopping and cooking are critical to any student settling in, and particularly if they struggle to make friends (as cooking for flatmates is a good way of meeting people) or are feeling low (when they may lose their appetite). In both cases, having a plan is important, so have fun developing manageable ones for each of these situations. Dealing with these areas can help a student manage situations of sensory and social overload and build towards more complex situations such as conferences, so they are critical skill areas to develop.

- From the outset, discuss with students their aims and goals following university so that they become familiar with this approach to planning for future options following their course.

Chapter 18:
Money management

This is an area that many students find problematic for a range of reasons, for example:

- not having managed their own money before, and not knowing how to budget

- not having handled a large sum of money before i.e. student finance money

- getting behind on payments, for example rent

- having debts to pay off and not knowing how to manage this

- responding to pressure from debtors

- not knowing who to talk to about finances.

Both your mentor and the student finance team are here to help you.

**Deal with problems sooner
rather than later to reduce stress.**

You can plan your monthly income and expenditure using Excel if that is easier for you. Do this with someone you trust, such as the university financial advice team, your mentor, a family member. It will help you see how much money you will have available to spend each month.

Bank accounts

It is really useful for you to have a bank account in your own name which you manage, as this enables you to be more independent.

Bank statements

A sample bank statement   20 July 2019

Account Type:		Current
Account Name:		Jo Bloggs
Account Number:		84678299
Branch Sort Code:		20-13-87

Date	Transaction type	Balance brought forward	Money In	Money Out	Balance
21st June					6430.00
22nd June	ATM* cash withdrawal			20.00	6430.00
24th June	DD* rent			2000.00	4430.00
26th June	SO* contents insurance			10.00	4420.00
1st July	ATM* cash withdrawal			10.00	4410.00
10th July	ATM* cash withdrawal			40.00	4370.00
19th July	CR* Birthday present		100.00		4470.00
		Balance Carried Forward			4470.00

*Cash machine (ATM)   *Direct Debit (DD) *Standing Order (SO) *Credit (CR)

In the example above, the columns are as follows:

1. Date.

2. Type of transaction e.g. cash machine (ATM), standing order (SO), direct debit (DD) etc.

3. Who was paid (the column starts with the balance brought forward from the previous page and ends with that going forward to the next page). This example may include previous transactions to do with student grant or any employment. Your balance may be very different to this.

4. Money out.

5. Money in.

6. Balance.

Try to be familiar with your monthly statements. Notice what all the transactions relate to. Your statements can be accessed online or as a hard copy.

> **For ease of access, you can use online banking or an app on your phone. This gives you ready access to transactions throughout the day and will help you stay on top of your finances.**

Student loan

Your student grant from Student Finance England will be paid into your bank account, so be aware of when you receive this and keep an eye on regular payments such as rent. Note that in Scotland bursaries and loans (and DSA) are dealt with by SAAS: http://www.saas.gov.uk/forms_and_guides/dsa.htm.

Sometimes difficulties can be encountered as the following quote by a student shows, but there are people who can help, so do remember to speak to someone as soon as an issue arises or you are not sure of something. This example provided by one student shows how support from a mentor, other staff and a family member helped them acquire finance for their course:

> 'I found it incredibly hard to fill out forms for my student loan and communication with them was not always easy. I didn't receive the correct maintenance loan in my second year and in my third year I didn't receive any at all for the first half of the academic year. This made me really struggle for money and not having the security and knowledge of when my money was going to come in was really

stressful. When contacting them about this they told me the same information each time: that my student declaration signature was lost. They didn't offer any alternative support and didn't take my disability into consideration. Luckily with the support from a staff member I was able to receive my full loan entitlement. Now I have finished my degree I am being contacted again saying I have overpayments that need to be paid right away which I find incredibly stressful. I think they can improve their ways in which they communicate with students especially disabled students and those who suffer with their mental health. Also they should make reasonable adjustments for those who are struggling. Luckily with helpful members of staff from my faculty and my mentor, mum and partner I was able to find the students loan system that little bit easier throughout my time at university.'

Personal Independence Payment

This is a tax free disability benefit divided into two parts; daily living and mobility. If you have made an application for Personal Independence Payment (PIP), you will be assessed for both. If successful, you will receive PIP payments at 4 weekly intervals.

If you do not receive PIP and have NOT made an application for it, you may wish to consider doing so. Your disability support worker/student finance staff and your mentor will all be able to help with this process.

There is no guarantee that you will be successful, but it is worth seeking advice from people such as your parents, your disability support worker, your GP or your medical consultant in relation to any disability as they will be able to support you with your application/provide relevant medical information.

Universal credit

Universal credit has now been rolled out across all areas of the UK and replaces the following benefits:

- housing benefit
- income support
- child tax credit
- income-based jobseeker's allowance (JSA)
- income-related employment and support allowance (ESA)
- working tax credit.

If you are a full-time student, you can't normally claim universal credit, but there are some exceptions to this rule. To check your eligibility look at: https://www.disabilityrightsuk.org/how-we-can-help/individuals/education/frequently-asked-questions-students.

Managing daily expenditure

Living on a student income can be challenging for most students, so it is important to regularly check your expenditure and income using the following methods:

- ATM cash machine.

- Online banking or an app.

- Hard copy statements (weekly or monthly).

If you are someone who spends money regularly and perhaps have a tendency to lose track of this, online banking or apps provide immediate easy access to your account. You can check your balance BEFORE purchases so that you do not run up any debts and spend more money than you have.

Hardship fund

If you are experiencing financial difficulties, visit the finance team. They have access to a range of information about funding possibilities to help support you as a student. These range from a 'hardship fund' to trusts that support disabled students. Here is one student's experience, which turned out well with mentoring support:

> 'I was lucky enough to be told about the hardship fund through my previous mentor, and my most recent mentor helped me complete the process. I wouldn't have known about it or been able to complete the application easily without their support. I myself find forms and anything to do with money stressful and organising all the different bits of information. So to have a mentor there to motivate me and help with things was really beneficial, I also had help from a member of the advice team in the student's union which helped push my application forward. I hope they advertise this to more students who are in need, such as those who struggle with their mental health and problems at home. I think they should especially advertise to disabled students as we don't get much from DSA throughout our whole three years at university. I hope they change the format of the forms as it was not clear how to fill it out and how to collect the relevant evidence. So hopefully there will be consideration in the future for those who find it difficult to fill out forms.'

> **If experiencing financial difficulties, the sooner you talk to someone, the sooner you can get help. You are not alone.**

Scholarships and bursaries

Both of these will open up various opportunities for you in terms of your study, for example, assisting you to travel abroad for part of your studies. Talk to your course leader or student finance team for more information.

Tips for mentors and study skills support workers

- Discussing opening their own bank account which students learn to manage can be very liberating for some, but cause distress for others, so this requires a sensitive approach.

- Flagging up to students the range of financial support at university is important to alleviating stress. Students come from a diversity of backgrounds, an increasing number have been homeless, many will come from backgrounds where they are struggling financially, and some may simply have not managed their own finances before for whatever reason.

- Introducing a proactive approach to money management is hugely important, whether it means avoiding debt or managing it, and educating students that it can be managed is a key life skill to impart.

- Build a general knowledge of the benefits system as it is invaluable if you are going to be able to advise the range of students you are asked to work with. Also know where to signpost to in your area for extra help e.g. Citizens' Advice Bureau.

- Knowledge about accessing the hardship fund, how to fill in the form or signpost to the finance team, is crucial as it may be something that is urgently required and the distress this situation causes may mean that students are less able to process information.

Chapter 19:
Employment

Your CV

Maintaining an up-to-date CV is essential if you are to be ready for the job market. As many different opportunities regarding employment and the job market will arise throughout your course, being prepared is an effective way of managing any stress or anxiety that may arise because of this. It enables you to:

- be clear about goals
- establish a strong set of skills
- build on knowledge gaps.

Activity 19.1: Building activities and work experience

Voluntary work is really useful for building on a range of skills. Check in your area for local voluntary organisations as this will help you to choose where you would like to work. Voluntary work is important for a variety of reasons:

- Helping you to build your confidence.
- Helping you with networking; this is invaluable when you move into the employment sector or need to find a work placement.
- Development of new skills in a variety of areas that will compliment or add to your main skill set.
- Providing you with additional CV material.

Activity 19.2: Skills audit

There are three main skill types:

- **Transferrable**, where skills learnt in one area of work can be adapted to another.
- **Job-specific**, where the skills and qualifications relate to a certain job.
- **Adaptive**, these are reflected by personality traits as opposed to experience.

Other skills you may have:

First aid qualification	Photo editing
Leadership	Time management
Team building	Organisational

Risk assessment

Event planning

Money-handling

ICT

Independent working/learning

Problem solving

Data handling

Patience under strenuous conditions

Customer care

Responsible and professional attitude

DBS checked

Teaching

Setting goals and objectives

Tutoring and understanding others' problems

Listening

Mentoring

Working with specific types of people e.g. children, young blind people etc

Contributing and sharing ideas

Performing

Managing people

Following instructions

Communication

It is important to include transferrable and job-specific skills on a CV as they help you stand out from other candidates.

The careers advisors at your university will help you develop and build your CV and can be contacted via student services. There are also many online resources to help you write a good CV.

Activity 19.3: Researching the field

Knowing what is happening in your area of research or work, and who the key players are, is key to you developing your work. Spend time looking these employers or researchers up and taking notes. You could ask yourself the following types of questions:

■ Who do you like/agree with? Why?

■ Who do you dislike/disagree with? Why?

■ Who would you like to work for? Why?

Activity 19.4: Setting up a LinkedIn account

You may want to do this activity as a way of linking with others, although for some of you it may be an activity that is part of your course. It requires setting up a profile of your work, and you can add as many or little other areas as you like e.g. education, publications, membership of professional bodies, skills, publications.

Activity 19.5: Finding a work placement

This is something you may wish to do with your mentor, although many student departments will have someone responsible for circulating information about current work placements and employment. Make sure that you are connected to this person as they can also help you identify your specific areas of interest and strength and ensure that you receive the most appropriate work links.

Activity 19.6: Applying for a job

Every university will have a department that provides careers advice and guidance. Check out the individual advice leaflets they put out on subjects such as:

- CVs
- covering letter
- job application
- searching the job market
- searching the hidden job market.

In addition to this, there will also be drop-in sessions where you can book to meet with a careers advisor. You can also take your mentor along with you to help/support you if you wish.

Interview skills

Careers departments at universities run sessions around various aspects of interviews. These also include:

- interviews on Skype
- employability
- Great with Disability, a website which provides advice for disabled students regarding a pathway to employment
- tests
- lists of typical interview questions so that you can reflect on these and practise answers (see Activity 19.5 above).

In addition, remember that at an interview you are also able to ask your own questions, so make sure that you have a couple ready. Here are some suggestions:

■ Look on the company website and check areas that you may wish to know more about.

■ Think about your skills, and ask them what opportunities there are for developing these further (known as continuing professional development, or CPD).

■ Is there something that the company does that you would be particularly interested in? For example attendance at training or conferences.

Presentations

Many interviews require you to do a presentation. Everyone has a different way of preparing presentations, so it is a matter of exploring what works for you. You can practise with your mentor or someone from the careers team at your university.

Use the following, individually or with your mentor, to think through your ideas and to boost your confidence:

■ At university, you will have done presentations for various modules, so on paper map the skills you have learnt.

■ Think about what the job you have applied for actually entails.

■ If the job asks for a presentation on a specific subject, map out the points you would like to make. It's easier if these are visual than as thoughts as you may be able to make better links.

■ Using PowerPoint make your **header slide** the title of the presentation, your name and email contact if you wish.

■ Put each **key point** you would like to talk about on a separate slide (you can think about the design later).

■ Look at your mind maps, and put the **points you have raised under these key headings**. Try not to have more than about 4-5 points per slide.

■ You can rearrange the order of your slides until they make better sense when you read them out loud.

■ You are now ready to design your slides.

   ■ Font: not less than 18 and possibly Arial, Verdana or Tahoma.

- Background colour is important for many autistic/neurodivergent individuals: see what suits you best, but as this is an interview try to select something that is professional.
- Slide layout: choose one that is not too distracting and allows your audience to focus on what you are saying.
- Images: perhaps select a few to enhance what you are saying.

Activity 19.7: Matching your skills to the job

Your university may produce a list of typical interview questions, or you can source some online. Keep an updated file with answers to these questions, so that you can practice these regularly.

Activity 19.8: Preparing for the interview

Preparing thoroughly beforehand is a key part in your success at interview.

- Research the company/organisation so that you can demonstrate some knowledge and prepare yourself with some questions.
- Practice your presentation either in front of someone or to yourself. Looking at yourself in a mirror may be helpful.
- First impressions are important at interviews, so think about how you are going to dress. You need to wear something formal but comfortable.
- Prepare your travel route to the interview well in advance.
- Consider asking someone to support you by travelling to the interview with you (they can always wait in a café nearby).

Activity 19.9: Accessing monetary support after graduation.

Accommodation

Many students become distressed about how they will manage money after graduation, so advice to ease the transition might be helpful.

With your mentor, list various options regarding accommodation, for example:

- Moving back home (this may not be an option for all students).
- Continuing in present, independent accommodation.
- Moving from student accommodation into independent accommodation (separately, or with friends).

- Moving into a friend's house.

- Moving into a hostel if you have previously been homeless.

- Any other options.

You can also visit the accommodation team/student services to discuss possible options.

Against each option, identify how you will finance paying the rent:

- Through work (be it short or long-term).

- Through Universal Credit benefit payments.

General living

As above, will this be funded through work, part-time, full-time or temporary?

Will you be applying for Universal Credit?

The earlier you can think these options through, the sooner you can put plans into place, such as applying for work or benefits, or moving back home.

Tips for mentors and study skills support workers

- From the outset, encourage your students to build a CV. Each university will have an expert careers department to advise, or you can discuss this initially with the student to produce a draft, as this will then be easier for them to discuss.

- Introduce activities/discussions about the students' future career from time to time, but be aware that this may be anxiety-provoking for some as processing course work (current focus) and thinking about the future at the same time can be challenging.

- Show students where they can find resources for writing covering letters and job applications and encourage them to familiarise themselves with these. Many won't wish to practise this skill until a real situation has arisen as hypothetical situations can be difficult to deal with, so just be aware of this.

- Constantly reviewing skills can be confidence-building and also highlight where a student needs to focus on new opportunities, so build this into your sessions.

- Encourage students to book regular careers sessions, particularly if they have to do work placements. You could discuss accompanying them if necessary. They will be given websites to look at and you can support them in this activity.

■ If a student successfully obtains an interview, discuss whether they want to send the organisation an email regarding reasonable adjustments for them. If so, you can offer to help them with this. Alternatively, they may wish you to do this on their behalf.

■ Source some typical interview questions and work with your students to write a short answer to each.

■ Linking course work and employment is important as this can be difficult for students, so including an understanding as to why the identification of key players in the field is critical, both for dissertations and following a course, is key to building future success in employment.

■ Encourage students to think about and plan future possibilities with you as soon as possible to reduce anxiety. Issues to address are accommodation, finance and employment or further study.

Chapter 20:
Further study

Following your degree, there are a number of different further study options available to you, and it is useful to be familiar with these so that you can reflect on them throughout your course.

Identifying further opportunities

Continue studies at current university

Some advantages of this choice are:

- Already being familiar with the environment/staff, so there is less change.
- You may already have a disability support worker and mentor, and these can remain the same.
- You have time to reflect on areas of your course and support that worked for you or where adjustments need to be made. This gives you more control over how you access a course.
- As there is less change, you may be able to adapt other areas of your life and consider independent living in student accommodation if you are not already doing so.

Continue studies at a new university

This choice allows you to:

- explore a new learning environment – they are all different in some way
- become more independent
- learn to adapt more readily to change, and build your skills and confidence
- develop a wider set of networks (friendship and work-related).

Have a gap year

Many students are undecided as to what to do next, or simply exhausted by having finished one course in the first place. This option allows you to manage anxiety about not knowing what to do next and provides time to do the following:

- Reflect on learning.
- Develop other skills.
- Network.

- Develop friendships.
- Consider other learning or employment opportunities available.
- Explore different environments locally, regionally, nationally and internationally.

Open University (OU) course

If the demands of an ordinary university were perhaps too overwhelming in terms of sensory and social overload, or you simply would like a learning environment that is more suited to your requirements, this option may be for you. The OU has around 150 distance learning courses or an 'open programme', where you can tailor the course to your requirements. Courses have:

- a number of tutors
- tutorials
- student forums
- online material
- plenty of support.

Both study and payment options are flexible, so you may find that this option is more suitable for you, especially if you have some days where you have far more energy to engage in your course than other days. This way you do not have the pressure of falling behind others on your course.

Online courses

There are many online courses, and several of these are free. You could ask your university for more details (e.g. your tutors or course leader or careers at student services) or use the Google search engine to track down something you like. It may be helpful to discuss ideas and potential choices with a familiar person (e.g. family or your mentor). In addition, your mentor/academic support worker will be familiar with your learning style and may be able to make recommendations or signpost you to someone who is best suited to do so.

Local courses

If you feel more comfortable studying locally, there may be a range of educational establishments around. For example, the Workers' Education Association (WEA) have many courses, and these vary throughout the year. In addition, courses run at different times of the day, and this may suit you better.

Adult education classes are set up at various institutions and have a diverse range of courses which you can access for fun or to obtain another qualification. Another option is language schools or arts centres as both provide a different type of course.

Continuing study whilst working

You may need to work as you study, and there are many courses around that allow you to do this, both distance and local. You may also be able to access different funding sources, for example your employer may fund your studies while you train with them.

Continue studies abroad

This can be an exciting option for those of you wishing to travel and build new contacts. Your present university may have links with international ones which can facilitate the process, or you may have built up your own links.

Activity 20.1: Mapping out choices

From this list of options, talk through the choices that interest you with a family member, your tutor or your mentor.

- List the advantages of each that interests you.
- List the disadvantages.
- Look at the expenditure and how you could fund this.
- Check out accommodation.
- If considering studying abroad, how well do you speak the language, and what support is there for you?
- If studying abroad, Student Finance England do not fund these courses, so what options are available to you? Go to the careers/finance at your current university and ask.
- Are there any bursaries or scholarships for study abroad, and especially for disabled students?
- Reflect on which seems to be the best choice for you.
- Check the application process, and if eligible and you are sure this is the course you would like to do next, then apply. You can always change your mind if you are offered a place.

Tips for mentors and study skills support workers

■ Including regular conversations into your sessions regarding future study or work enables students to process information at their own pace and not suddenly towards the end of their course.

■ I believe the key to dealing with this area successfully is to introduce discussing each option as a fun opportunity as opposed to a threat. Visiting places online, or suggesting that students may wish to access prospectuses for extended courses is one way of doing this. Remember, informed choices help reduce anxiety.

■ Constructing a 'future possibilities that I like' portfolio may assist students as it is a reflective tool. Writing the reasons for these preferences alongside will help the students process their thoughts, and particularly if they change as they progress through their course.

Chapter 21:
Autism research, activities and the autistic community

Around the university, there may well be some spaces that you find quieter, less bright, or which suit your needs in some other way. It is important that you identify these as they will change according to whether other students have exams or dissertations and wish to study in the library or around other campus areas.

If you do not find spaces that can work for you, this can lead to you working from home or in your room and further isolating yourself from others. Ask your mentor to help you look around for these spaces, and you will probably have more flexibility if you have a laptop through DSA.

In addition, you may feel you would like to connect to the wider autistic community involved in activities and research established by autistic people for autistic people.

There is an eclectic mix of resources for you to access according to your preferences, and these include: books, websites, research groups, journals, residentials, organisations, and tools. The following is not an exhaustive list, but serves to introduce you to some areas looking to put the autistic voice first in matters relating to autism, and I have provided one or two examples in each area. It is dealt with in the order given above.

Books

Both the References section and the Suggested Further Reading sections of this book signpost you to a range of different material, academic, biographical and autobiographical, which will inform your knowledge around a range of issues relating to autism, such as:

- personal experiences
- sensory sensitivity
- managing anxiety and stress
- tackling feelings of isolation
- disclosure
- employment
- self-help
- networking.

These resources all have the potential to act as a self-help guide with some aspects of your life, and I would particularly encourage you to access a wide range of resources written by different autistic individuals, as these can highlight the similarities and differences experienced and show you that you are not alone.

Websites

There are an increasing number of websites and blogs written on experiences from the perspective of an autistic person (diagnosed or self-diagnosed), on autism research and autism activism, among others. Of course each portrays autism differently, and accessing these can be a good way of helping you to express your identity or voice your experiences. The following are just three examples and there will also be others specific to your geographical area.

Wrongplanet
http://wrongplanet.net/

This website is a community for autistic individuals and those with other neurological conditions or differences.

With lots of very different comments, perspectives and ideas, this site will certainly get you thinking and perhaps encourage you to share some of your views. Building confidence to express our views is key to accepting, exploring and developing our identities.

Autistic Women's Collective
https://www.facebook.com/AWCollective/

The Autistic Women's Collective is an online space for autistic women and mothers of autistic daughters to connect, make friends, have a voice and find support.

The Autistic Women's Empowerment Project
https://www.facebook.com/AWCollective/Autistic Trans Community
https://www.facebook.com/search/str/autistic+trans+community/keywords_search

The Autistic Women's Empowerment Project (AWE) is a peer lead network for Autistic Women around the UK developing circles of support.

Research groups

Participatory Autism Research Collective (PARC)

PARC was set up 'to bring autistic people, including scholars and activists, together with early career researchers and practitioners who work with autistic people. Our aim is to build a community network where those who wish to see more significant involvement of autistic people in autism research can share knowledge and expertise'. To become involved, have a discussion, or to find out what is happening in your area or around the country, check out the website: https://participatoryautismresearch.wordpress.com/

Shaping Autism Research in the UK

Research from an earlier study, 'A future made together' (Pellicano *et al*, 2013), showed that the expressed experiences of autistic participants in studies were often dehumanising, so this project looked at ways of exploring this issue and seeking ways to address this through participatory research. This was done through five different seminars, which have produced resources, an archive of material and a research paper. As such, it is a positive step forward in bringing autistic and non-autistic individuals together to progress autism research which addresses the autistic agenda by putting the autistic voice at the heart of this process. You can read more about this here: http://www.shapingautismresearch.co.uk/.

This work resulted in further (participatory) research work on five themes: respect, authenticity, assumptions, infrastructure and empathy, to build participatory research skills among the autism research community and 'greater autistic leadership of, and partnership in, research' (Fletcher-Watson *et al*, 2018).

Journals

One example of an open access (free to access) online journal established by an autistic academic, Dr Larry Arnold particularly encourages the writings of autistic individuals.

Autonomy, the Critical Journal of Interdisciplinary Autism Studies
http://www.larry-arnold.net/Autonomy/index.php/autonomy/index

This online open access journal was established by Dr Larry Arnold. As an offshoot from the Autreach project, it is aimed at 'appealing to the widest range of the current autism research community' fostering links between a number of disciplines, for example medical research, education and sociology.

As a journal, Autonomy encourages autistic scholars to contribute, with submitted papers peer reviewed by respected academics in the field. It also includes two sections to stimulate debate, namely reviews and opinions.

Autism, Policy and Practice
https://www.openaccessautism.org/index.php/app/about

An online open access biannual journal that is autistic-led and aims to bridge the gap between theory, research and practice. The journal was re-initiated in 2018 with an autistic-led team and sets a standard by making adjustments to include and encourage neurodivergent authors and stakeholders whose voices would otherwise remain absent.

Residentials

Autscape
http://www.autscape.org/

Autscape is a three-day residential conference, which is created primarily for autistic participants and organised and run by autistic people. By allowing autistic individuals to retreat to an autistic-friendly space and relax away from mainstream society, an opportunity is provided for individuals to meet socially, join in with conference talks, workshops and advocacy, and to do as much or as little networking as they wish.

With autistic individuals taking the lead on organisation and presenting, and with the majority of participants being autistic, this is a conference with a difference. Autistic behaviour and communication preferences are encouraged and respected and as much attention as possible is given to organisation and planning in terms of preparing a varied schedule of relaxed and more organised activities within a more relaxed environment. Check out the website to look at past and present Autscapes.

Organisations

ARGH (Autistic Rights Group Highland)
http://www.arghighland.co.uk/index.html

Run by and for autistic adults, this is a collective advocacy, lobbying and campaigning group of autistic adults in the Highlands and beyond. ARGH informs service providers about the real lived experiences of autistics; campaigns for improved services for autistics living in and beyond the highlands; and challenges all stigma and discrimination of autistics by educating non-autistics about autistic strengths. It is currently free to join, although welcomes donations, and ARGH meetings are only open to members. All members have an autistic spectrum condition.

Tools

ASK
http://www.autisticspacekit.co.uk

The Autistic Space Kit is an app develop by autistic people to help autistic individuals cope in moments of stress and to communicate their requirements.

With convenient 'buttons' for medical and space for alert card information, this app also allows users to edit the globally recognised red, yellow and green interaction timers to suit their requirements. The app also provides scope to introduce pre-prepared scripts to help manage anxiety, and it can update selected contacts as to your location, should support be needed when stressed.

Tips for mentors and study skills support workers

- Do inform yourself (and your student if they are unaware of these and wish to know) about the autistic community, research and online and local activities.

- Be prepared to ask what your students know about the autistic community, research and online and local activities. It's often fun to discuss these.

- Do identify autism-friendly spaces within the university that you work. If there are none, you may wish to discuss this with the disability team as they have a responsibility to address this under the Equality Act (2010).

- Many autistic students experience isolation, so familiarising them with books, discussion groups, autism-friendly conferences and other resources named in this section is an empowering way to tackle this. Knowing that they are not alone is a powerful feeling, so encourage students to develop their knowledge in this area.

Chapter 22: Organisations/contacts you may find helpful

Under each of these headings, I offer a suggested service that has a national or local organisation. You would be able to contact either, and they should be able to signpost you to someone else if necessary. Either way, if you need support, there are many individuals and organisations available to help.

Black and Minority Ethnic Groups (BAME)

AUVoice
www.autismvoice.org.uk

Based in South London, AUVoice works with families and people on the autism spectrum in this region. The goal is to tackle and end stigma and discrimination attached to autism.

NUS Black Students
https://www.nus.org.uk/en/who-we-are/how-we-work/black-students/

Focusing on issues affecting black students, this is a local and national campaigning group representing students of African, Asian, Arab and Caribbean descent.

Mental Health Foundation (MHF)
https://www.mentalhealth.org.uk/a-to-z/b/black-asian-and-minority-ethnic-bame-communities

Generally, people from BAME groups living in the UK are more likely to experience mental health problems and this reflects their cultural heritage and appropriate treatment. The MHF provides useful information and support.

The Transformation Fund Legacy
http://www.transformationfund.org.uk/explore/who/black-and-minority-ethnic-groups

This organisation funds projects that specifically address BAME issues.

Disability

Disability Rights UK
https://www.disabilityrightsuk.org/

This organisation provides lots of useful information about disabilities and disabled people's rights. In addition, it looks at those rights in the context of the higher education environment and reasonable adjustments.

NAS (National Autistic Society)

With over 700,000 people in the UK on the autism spectrum, and many undiagnosed, it is essential that inclusive services are established and autism awareness remains firmly on the agenda. As a national organisation, the NAS was the first established to address this and was initially led by non-autistic parents. However, it now exists alongside numerous regional and advocacy groups, many of which are autistic-led.

Mental health services/counselling

Child and Adolescent Mental Health Services (CAMHS)

Depending on where you live, CAMHS may be a service that can provide you with support if you have mental health needs as they work with young people up to 25 years of age.

MIND

MIND provide advice and support to anyone experiencing a mental health problem. In addition, they campaign to improve services, raise awareness and promote understanding of any aspect related to mental well-being.

Samaritans

As a non-religious organisation, the Samaritans provide a 24-hour service to contact if you need to talk about problems you are facing. It is a safe place for you to talk in your own way.

LGBT services

Gender, Identity, Research and Education Society (GIRES)

http://www.gires.org.uk/

Gires' mission is to improve the lives of trans and gender non-conforming people, including those who are non-binary and non-gender, by working with them to give a voice and also working with families. It is a volunteer-led charity which works to educate and guide research in this area.

LGBT Foundation

http://lgbt.foundation/information-advice/sexual-violence/

An organisation tackling many areas and with a focus on the LGBT community.

LGBT Resource Centre Gender Pronouns

https://uwm.edu/lgbtrc/support/gender-pronouns/

Stonewall

http://www.stonewall.org.uk/

Stonewall works to let all lesbian, gay, bi and trans people, in the UK and abroad, know they are not alone. In order to achieve this, they partner with other organisations to work for change. They feel their work will only be done when everyone can feel free to be who they are regardless of context.

Warwick (Equality, Diversity and Inclusion) (2019) Pronouns: Let's get it right

https://warwick.ac.uk/services/equalops/transandgenderreassignment/getpronounsright

Rape and sexual violence support

Rape and Sexual Violence Project

Through the provision of a counselling and advocacy service to survivors of sexual abuse and domestic violence, RSVP enable individuals to overcome the effects of sexual/domestic violence. This can enable changes for a positive future. Support is also offered through an independent sexual violence advocate (ISVA) to provide support and guidance through all aspects of a court case if wished.

Sexual health

http://www.nhs.uk/livewell/sexualhealthtopics/pages/sexual-health-hub.aspx

This site tells you about sexual health, contraception and sexually transmitted diseases (STIs) and what is available in your area.

VictimFocus

https://www.victimfocus.org.uk/about-us

Owned by Dr Jessica Eaton, VictimFocus embraces the VictimFocus blog and the Eaton Foundation to critically explore child sexual exploitation, victim blaming, feminism, sexual violence and also male mental health. Plenty of resources are provided.

Women's Aid

https://www.womensaid.org.uk/

This organisation places women at its heart and focuses on domestic violence, including rape and sexual abuse. In addition, further support is given with issues such as harassment and stalking.

Tips for mentors and study skills support workers

- The students you are allocated to support will bring a diversity of challenges, not just that/those highlighted on their support statement. For this reason it is essential that you are familiar with a range of external services in your locality that you can signpost to.

- Remember, students experiencing specific challenges may not wish to access support on campus, so be prepared to ask students if they would like information and then to offer it. Examples of this might be mental health services or specialist rape support services as accessing these on campus can interfere with a student's ability to focus on course work.

- Certain communities and individuals are reluctant to accept disabilities, different abilities or different identities, and this provides a different layer of stress for students. Be sensitive to this, discuss this if the student wishes and talk about signposting to other services e.g. the local LGBTQ+ centre.

- Always be prepared to raise conversations, not in a voyeuristic fashion, but as a means to assisting the voicing of experiences.

- Regardless of whether you are skilled or comfortable with dealing with certain areas, make sure that you know who is around to support you e.g. the safeguarding protocol, the mental health support available in the university where you work, this may include rape and sexual violence support as universities are increasingly responding to this need.

References

References

Beresford P (2005) 'Service user': regressive or liberatory terminology? *Disability and Society* **20** (4) 469-477.

Black A (2012) *Living in the Moment: Don't dwell on the past or worry about the future...simply be in the present.* London: CICO Books.

Bornstein K (2013) *My New Gender Workbook: A step-by-step guide to achieving world peace through gender anarchy and sex positivity.* London: Routledge.

Copeland ME (2016) *Wellness Recovery Action Plan (WRAP)* [online]. Available at: http://mentalhealthrecovery.com/wrap-is/ (accessed December 2017).

Department of Health (2010a) *Fulfilling and Rewarding Lives: The strategy for adults with autism in England* [online]. Available at: http://webarchive. nationalarchives.gov.uk/20130104203954/http://www.dh.gov.uk/en/ Publicationsandstatistics/Publications/PublicationsPolicyAndGuidance/ DH_113369 (accessed December 2017).

Department of Health (2010b) *Implementing "Fulfilling and Rewarding Lives": Statutory guidance for local authorities and NHS organisations to support implementation of the autism strategy* [online]. Available at: https://www.gov.uk/ government/uploads/system/uploads/attachment_data/file/216129/dh_122908. pdf (accessed December 2017).

Department of Health (2014) *Think Autism: Fulfilling and Rewarding Lives, the strategy for adults with autism in England: an update* [online]. Social Care, Local Government and Care Partnership Directorate, Department of Health. Available at: https://www.gov.uk/government/uploads/system/uploads/attachment_data/ file/299866/Autism_Strategy.pdf (accessed December 2017).

Eaton J (2019) *Critical Perspectives: Child sexual exploitation approaches and practice.* UK: VictimFocus Publications.

Fletcher-Watson S, Adams J, Brook K, Charman T, Crane L, Cusack J, Leekam S, Milton D, Parr JR and Pellicano E (2018) Making the future together: shaping autism research through meaningful participation. *Autism: International Journal of Research and Practice* **23** (4).

Graby S (2012) *To Be or Not to Be Disabled: Autism, disablement and identity politics.* Presented at the 'Theorising Normalcy and the Mundane' conference, 27th June 2012, University of Chester.

Jackson J (2006) Disclosure: A parent's perspective. In: D Murray (Ed.) *Coming Out Asperger: diagnosis, disclosure and self-diagnosis.* London: Jessica Kingsley Publishers.

Kenny L, Hattersley C, Molins B, Buckley C, Povey C & Pellicano E (2015) Which terms should be used to describe autism? Perspectives from the UK autism community. *Autism* **20** (4) 442–462.

Krueger J (2015) *Flow and Happiness: Do you have to be an expert to be happy?* [online] Psychology Today. Available at: https://www.psychologytoday.com/blog/one-among-many/201502/flow-and-happiness (accessed December 2017).

Lawson W (2005) *Sex, Sexuality and the Autism Spectrum.* London: Jessica Kingsley Publishers.

Lawson W (2006a) Coming out, various. In: D Murray (Ed.) *Coming Out Asperger: Diagnosis, disclosure and self-confidence.* London, Jessica Kingsley Publishers.

Lawson W (2006b) *Friendships: The aspie way.* London: Jessica Kingsley Publishers.

Milton D (2012) On the ontological status of autism: the double empathy problem. *Disability and Society* **27** (6) 883–887.

Moxon L (2006) Diagnosis, disclosure and self-confidence in sexuality and relationships. In: D Murray (Ed.) *Coming Out Asperger: Diagnosis, disclosure and self-confidence.* London, Jessica Kingsley Publishers.

Murray D (Ed.) (2006) *Coming Out Asperger: Diagnosis, disclosure and self-confidence.* London: Jessica Kingsley Publishers.

Pellicano E, Dinsmore A and Charman T (2013) A Future Made Together: Shaping autism research in the UK. London, Institute of Education.

Research Autism (2015) *Cygnet Project: Mentoring scheme for young people with autism spectrum conditions* [online]. Available at: http://researchautism.net/cygnet-project. London: Research Autism.

Ridout S and Edmondson M (2017) Cygnet mentoring project: combined experiences from a mentor and a mentee. *Autonomy, the Critical Journal of Interdisciplinary Autism Studies* **1** (5).

Robinson KS (2010) *Bring on the Learning Revolution!* [online]. Available at: http://www.ted.com/talks/sir_ken_robinson_bring_on_the_revolution.html (accessed December 2017).

Robinson SK (2006) *Do Schools Kill Creativity?* [online]. Available at: www.youtube.com/watch?v=iG9CE55wbtY (accessed December 2017).

Shore S (2006) Disclosure: Talking about what makes us human. In: D Murray (Ed.) *Coming Out Asperger: Diagnosis, disclosure and self-confidence.* London: Jessica Kingsley Publishers.

Williams MA and Penman D (2011) *Mindfulness: A practical guide to finding peace in a frantic world.* London: Piatkus.

Suggested further reading

Andrews M (2014a) *Narrative Imagination and Everyday Life.* Oxford: Oxford University Press.

Andrews P (2014b) *Autistic Participation in Widening Access to Higher Education. Participation and inclusion from the inside out: seeing autism from an autistic perspective.* London: NAS and Ask Autism.

ARGH and HUG (2011) *Autism and Mental Health: The views of people on the autistic spectrum on their mental health needs and mental health services* [online]. Inverness: ARGH (Autistic Rights Group Highland) and HUG (Action for Mental Health). Available at: http://www.arghighland.co.uk/pdf/arghhug.pdf (accessed December 2017).

Arnold L (2012) Autism, its relationship to science and to people with the condition. *Autonomy, the Critical Journal of Interdisciplinary Autism Studies* **1** (1).

Autism-Europe (2014) *Autism and Work: Together we can* [online]. Brussels: Autism-Europe. Available at: http://www.autismeurope.org/wp-content/uploads/2017/08/waad-2014-press-release-en.pdf (accessed December 2017).

Autscape (2013) *Concept: What is Autscape?* [online]. Available at: http://www.autscape.org/about/concept. Cambridge: The Autscape Organisation (accessed December 2017).

Autscape (2015) *Exploring Autistic Space* [online]. Available at: http://www.autscape.org/2015/AutscapeInfo%2015.2-programme.pdf. North Yorkshire: Autscape (accessed December 2017).

Baker DL (2006) Neurodiversity, neurological disability and the public sector: notes on the autism spectrum. *Disability and Society* **21** (1) 15–29.

Baker MJ and Gabb J (2016) *The Secrets of Enduring Love: How to make relationships last.* London: Vermilion.

Barnes C and Mercer G (2013) *Exploring Disability* (2nd edition). Cambridge: Polity Press.

Beardon L, Martin N & Woolsey I (2009) What do students with Asperger syndrome or high functioning autism want at college and university? (in their own words). *Good Autism Practice* **10** (2) 35–43.

Bloxall K and Beresford P (2013) Service user research in social work and disability studies in the united kingdom. *Disability and Society* **28** (5) 587–600.

Booth J (2016) *Autism Equality in the Workplace.* London: Jessica Kingsley Publishers.

Bracher MJ (2013) *Living Without a Diagnosis – Formations of pre-diagnostic identity in the lives of as people diagnosed in adulthood.* PhD, Southampton.

Brown P, Davies J & Ridout S (2015) *Autism and Higher Education.* Presentation to staff at Birmingham Conservatoire.

Butt T (2007) Personal construct theory and method: another look at laddering. *Persona; Construct Theory and Practice* **4** 11–14.

CodeClan (2016) *Get Ready to Create Code* [online]. Available at: https://codeclan.com/ Edinburgh: CodeClan (accessed December 2017).

Crenshaw K (1991) Mapping the margins: intersectionality, identity politics, and violence against women of color. *Stanford Law Review* **43** (6) 1241–1299.

Croft S, Bewley C, Beresford P, Branfield F, Fleming J, Glynn M & Postle K (2011) *Person-Centred Support: A guide to person-centred working for practitioners.* London, Shaping Our Lives, The Joseph Rowntree Foundation.

Cummins RA (2013) Personal well-being index – adult (PWI-A). 5th ed. In: *Personal Wellbeing Index – Adult (PWI-A).* IW Group, Melbourne, Australian Centre on Quality of Life, Deakin University. Available at: http://www.acqol.com.au/iwbg/wellbeing-index/pwi-a-english.pdf (accessed December 2017).

Eddo-Lodge R (2017) *Why I'm No Longer Talking to White People About Race Anymore.* London: Bloomsbury Publishing.

Edmonds G and Beardon L (2008) *Asperger Syndrome and Employment: Adults speak out about Asperger syndrome.* London: Jessica Kingsley Publishers.

Edmondson M (2016) *Help Matthew Learn to Code!* https://www.gofundme.com/x8k2j658

EHRC (2017) *Public Sector Equality Duty* [online]. London: Equality and Human Rights Commission (EHRC). Available at: https://www.equalityhumanrights.com/en/advice-and-guidance/public-sector-equality-duty (accessed December 2017).

Fabri M, Andrews PCS & Pukki H (2016) Best practice for professionals supporting autistic students within or outside HE institutions. In Programme LL (Ed.). Available at: https://www.autism-uni.org (accessed December 2017).

Fairclough N (Ed) (2009) *A Dialectical-relational Approach to Clinical Discourse Analysis in Social Research.* London: SAGE Publications Ltd.

Forsythe L, Rahim N & Bell L (2008*) Benefits and Employment Support Schemes to Meet the Needs of People with an Autistic Spectrum Disorder.* London: Inclusion Research and Consultancy.

Garvey B, Stokes P & Megginson D (2009) *Coaching and Mentoring: Theory and Practice.* London: SAGE Publications Ltd.

Giles DC (2013) 'DSM-V is taking away our identity': the reaction of the online community to the proposed changes in the diagnosis of Asperger's disorder. *Health* 1–17.

Glover RA (2003) *No More Mr Nice Guy: A proven plan for getting what you want in love, sex and life.* Pennsylvania: Running Press Book Publishers.

Graby S (2015) Neurodiversity. In H Spandler, J Anderson & B Sapey (Eds) *Madness, Distress and the Politics of Disablement.* Bristol: Policy Press.

Henry D (2017) *Trans Voices: Becoming who you are.* London: Jessica Kingsley Publishers.

Hesmondhalgh M (2006) *Autism, Access and Inclusion on the Front Line: Confessions of an autism anorak.* London: Jessica Kingsley Publishers.

King R (2014) *How Autism Freed me to be Myself* [online]. Available at: http://www.ted.com/talks/rosie_king_how_autism_freed_me_to_be_myself?utm_source=twitterfeed&utm_medium=twitter&utm_campaign=Feed%3A+TEDTalks_video+%28TEDTalks+Main+%28SD%29+-+Site%29#t-75960 (accessed December 2017).

Lewthwaite S (2014) Cuts to grant funding for disabled students will put their studies at risk. *The Guardian* **24** April.

Mad People's History and Identity (2014) Eastspace: East Lothian Free Online Course. Available at: http://eastspace.org.uk/event/free-course-in-mad-peoples-history-and-identity/ (accessed December 2017).

Martin N (2011) Promoting inclusive practice for PhD students near completion. *Journal of Inclusive Practice in Further and Higher Education* **3** (2) 37–52

Meyerding J (2006) Coming out autistic at work. In: D Murray (Ed.) *Coming Out Asperger: Diagnosis, disclosure and self-esteem.* London, Jessica Kingsley Publishers.

Miller A (2002) *Mentoring students and young people: A handbook of effective practice.* Oxford: Routledge.

Mills R, NAS, *Research Autism & Francis J (2010) Access to Social Care and Support for Adults with Autistic Spectrum Conditions (ASC)* [online]. London, SCIE. Available at: http://www.autismrpphub.org/sites/default/files/resources/scie_access_to_social_care_and_support_for_adults_with_asc.pdf (accessed December 2017).

Milton D, Mills R & Jones S (2015) *Ten Rules for Ensuring People with Learning Disabilities and Those Who Are On The Autism Spectrum Develop 'Challenging Behaviour'…and maybe what to do about it.* Brighton: Pavilion Publishing & Media.

Milton D and Moon L (2012) The normalisation agenda and the psycho-emotional disablement of autistic people. *Autonomy, the Critical Journal of Interdisciplinary Autism Studies* **1** (1).

Milton D and Simms T (2015) The Research Autism Cygnet Mentoring Pilot Project: Mentor Training Day. Research Autism & London South Bank University.

Moon L (2014) *Under the Gaze: Fishbowling, commodification and lenses. Theorising autism.* Centre for Research in Autism and Education.

Murray D (ed.) (2006a) *Coming out Asperger: Diagnosis, disclosure and self-confidence.* London: Jessica Kingsley Publishers.

Murray D, Lesser M & Lawson W (2005) Attention, monotropism and the diagnostic criteria for autism. *Autism* **9** (2) 139–156.

NAO (2009) *Supporting People with Autism Through Adulthood.* London, NAO (National Audit Office).

NAS (1964) *Spell (Structure, Positive, Empathy, Low Arousal, Links)* [online]. Available at: http://www.autism.org.uk/about/strategies/spell.aspx London: NAS (accessed December 2017).

National Autistic Society (2011) *Untapped Talent: A guide to employing people with autism.* London, DWP & NAS.

NEF (2012) *Economics as if People and the Planet Really Mattered.* London: The New Economics Foundation.

Perry G (2014) *Playing to the Gallery.* London: Penguin Books Ltd.

Reeve D (2015) Psycho-emotional disablism in the lives of people experiencing mental distress. In: H Spandler, J Anderson & B Sapey (Eds) *Madness, Distress and the Politics of Disablement.* Bristol: Policy Press.

Research Autism (2015) *Cygnet Project: Mentoring Scheme for Young People with Autism Spectrum Conditions* [online]. Available at: http://researchautism. net/cygnet-project (accessed December 2017).

Ridout S (2016) *Narrating Experience: The Advantage of Using Mixed Expressive Media to Bring Autistic Voices to the Fore in Discourse Around Their Support Requirements.* Doctoral thesis, University of Birmingham.

Ridout S and Edmondson M (2017) Cygnet Mentoring Project: combined experiences from a mentor and a mentee. *Autonomy, the Critical Journal of Interdisciplinary Autism Studies* **1** (5).

Robinson SK (2006) *Do Schools Kill Creativity?* [online]. Available at: www. youtube.com/watch?v=iG9CE55wbtY (accessed December 2017).

Robertson SM (2010) Neurodiversity, quality of life, and autistic adults: shifting research and professional focuses onto real-life challenges. *Disability Studies Quarterly* **30**.

SFE (2016) *Non-Medical Help Services Reference Manual.* London: Student Finance England.

Shore S (2008) *Survival In The Workplace* [online]. Available at: http://www.asperger.it/?q=node/144 (accessed December 2017).

Slorach R (2016) *A Very Capitalist Condition: A history and politics of disability.* London: Bookmarks Publications.

Stoetzler M and Yuval-Davis N (2007) Standpoint theory, situated knowledge and the situated imagination. *Feminist Theory* **3** (3) 315–333.

Tantum D and Prestwood S (1999) *A Mind of One's Own: A guide to the special difficulties and needs of the more able person with autism or Asperger syndrome.* London: The National Autistic Society.

Teich NM (2012) *Transgender 101: A simple guide to a complex issue.* New York: Columbia University Press.

Walker N (2014) *Neurodiversity: Some basic terms and definitions* [online]. Neurocosmopolitanism: Nick Walker's notes on neurodiversity, autism and cognitive liberty. Available at: http://neurocosmopolitanism.com/neurodiversity-some-basic-terms-definitions/ (accessed December 2017).

Western S (2012) *Coaching and Mentoring: A critical text.* London: SAGE Publications Ltd.

Williams M, Coare P, Marvell R, Pollard E, Houghton A-M & Anderson J (2015) *Understanding Provision for Students with Mental Health Problems and Intensive Support Needs. Report to HEFCE by the Institute for Employment Studies (IES) and Researching Equity, Access and Partnership (REAP)* [online]. Institute for Employment Studies. Available at: http://www.hefce.ac.uk/media/HEFCE,2014/Content/Pubs/Independentresearch/2015/Understanding,provision,for,students,with,mental,health,problems/HEFCE2015_mh.pdf (accessed December 2017).

Williams M and Pollard E (2015) *Universities and Student Mental Health: How are universities coping with soaring demand?* [online]. Brighton Institute for Employment Studies. Available at: http://www.employment-studies.co.uk/news/universities-and-student-mental-health-how-are-universities-coping-soaring-demand (accessed December 2017).

Wrong Planet website: http://wrongplanet.net/.

Yergeau M (2010) Circle wars: reshaping the typical autism essay. *Disability Studies Quarterly* **30** (1).

Yuval-Davis N (2007) Intersectionality, citizenship and contemporary politics of belonging. *Critical Review of International Social and Political Philosophy* **10** (4) 561–574.

Appendices

Appendix 1: Example day planner

Day Planner

NB: Allocate some time for relaxation

Before 8am

8-9am

9-10am

10-11am

11am-12pm

12-1pm

1-2pm

2-3pm

3-4pm

4-5pm

5-6pm

After 6pm

Date:

Main tasks

To do if there's time

Notes

Appendix 2: Example weekly planner

Week Planner	For week beginning:	Monday	Tuesday	Wednesday	Thursday	Friday	Saturday	Sunday
Before 8am								
8-9am								
9-10am								
10-11am								
11am-12pm								
12-1pm								
1-2pm								
2-3pm								
3-4pm								
4-5pm								
5-6pm								
After 6pm								

Appendix 3: Characteristics of a good friend

Really important	Would be interesting	Would not like

Some suggestions that you may add to your lists are below. You could discuss this with your mentor.

Co-operative	Likes to cook
Good listener	Would support me if I had a problem
Likes to talk to people	Similar interests
Helpful	Would give advice sensitively if asked
Shares possessions	Interesting conversationalist
Shares time with others	Likes to visit galleries/cinema
Polite	Plays a sport
Trustworthy	Goes to a club/society

Appendix 4: Interests and activities

Rating your activities in terms of 1 (your favourite), with the highest number you allocate being your least favourite. You may add to and change the list according to your preferences.

	Rating
Attending a place of worship	
Bike riding	
ComicCon	
Computer time/internet	
Cooking for friends	
Eating out	
Pets	
Playing sports	
Playing video/computer games	
Reading	
Swimming	
Walking	
Watching movies/TV	
Watching sports	
Writing	
Other	

Appendix 5: Drawing your worries (an example)

Course work

- Do I understand it?
- Am I doing it right?
- My tutors don't understand me

Sensory sensitivity

- Overload
- Lights
- Rest breaks
- Finding a quiet area

Friends

- Feeling isolated
- Starting conversations
- Joining a group

Gender questioning

- Who can I talk to?
- Family response
- Am I normal?
- LGBTQ+ resources

Independent living

- Sharing a flat/house
- Money management
- Travel
- Cooking

Appendix 6: Intersectionality: some key terms

You may wish to add to these.

Accessibility

This is when an environment is open and available to people regardless of (dis)abilities. For example, equipment for people with hearing impairments in a conference room, availability of braille translations for people with visual impairments, or different lighting for those with light sensitivities (e.g. many people with epilepsy or who are autistic).

Cis (gender)

Someone whose self-identity matches with the gender that corresponds to their assigned gender; not trans.

Disability

This term covers both impairment and difference, and barriers to inclusion are highlighted by these. Often guided by negative language, conjuring up images of 'normality', the medical model of disability is a 'top down', 'expert-professional led' approach with an emphasis on the dysfunctional nature of disabled or differently abled individuals. The social model of disability places expertise within the individual, separating out impairments from services that are required by all.

Gender identity

Gender identity is a person's individual sense and experience of their own gender, for example male, female or non-binary.

Intersectionality

This entails the understanding that inequalities and oppression cross different identity categories, and a recognition that social identities are multi-dimensional. An example of how this may be seen is where sexual orientation and gender identity may be judged differently in relation to a number of other social subjectivities, such as age, ethnicity, region or country of origin.

Multiple discrimination

Discrimination based on two or more identities/intersections, such as religion or belief, race, disability, age, gender, gender identity and/or sexual orientation.

Power/privilege

A societal structure that provides people with more or less influence and conditions for influencing society and their own lives. An example of this is where the opportunities and conditions a person has are related to financial standing, sex and ethnicity.

Racial and ethnic identity

Racial and ethnic identity concerns membership of a particular cultural, national, or racial group that may share some of the following elements: culture, religion, race, language, or place of origin. Two people can share the same race but have different ethnicities.

Reasonable adjustments

A reasonable adjustment is made in a system to accommodate or make fair the same system for an individual based on a proven need, for example using lamps rather than fluorescent lighting.

Safe space

Safe space is a term for an area or forum where either a marginalised group are not supposed to face standard mainstream stereotypes and marginalisation, or in which a shared political or social viewpoint is required to participate in the space.

Sex

Sex refers to a person's biological status and is typically categorised as male, female, or intersex. There are a number of indicators of biological sex, including sex chromosomes, gonads, internal reproductive organs, and external genitalia.

Sexual orientation

Sexual orientation describes to whom someone is attracted. This includes attraction to the same gender (homosexual), opposite gender (heterosexual), and both genders (bisexual). Other orientations, often grouped under the term queer can include attraction to non-binary genders or genders which do not fit under traditional concepts of male or female.

Social model

The social model of (dis)ability is a reaction to the dominant medical model of (dis) ability which in itself is a functional analysis of the body as a machine to be fixed in order to conform with normative values. The social model is based on the premise that sensory, physical, intellectual, psychosocial and other impairments are met with physical, attitudinal, and institutional barriers in society and it is these barriers that hinder the full and effective participation of people with (dis)abilities.

Socio-economic status

Socioeconomic status is a societal construct that indicates an individual or group's social standing or class in respect to others in society. It is commonly measured by taking into consideration an individual or groups' education, income and occupation. There are three major categories referred to when allocating a socioeconomic status: high, middle, and low socioeconomic status.

Tokenism

This concerns situations where only a symbolic or the minimum effort to do a particular thing is carried out. This is often in relation to including a small number of people from under-represented, or disenfranchised, groups in order to give the appearance of full inclusion or diversity.

Trans

An umbrella term for people whose gender identity and/or gender expression differs from the sex assigned to them at birth. This term can include many gender identities such as: transsexual, transgender, crossdresser, drag performer, androgynous, genderqueer, gender variant or differently gendered people.

Appendix 7: Setting your agenda

Points for agenda	Feelings	Discussion/activity agreed
Past difficulties and experiences	■ Isolation ■ Confusion ■ Alienation ■ Rejection ■ Dysphoria	
Current encounters	■ Dysphoria ■ Relationships ■ Lack of confidence ■ Hateful comments ■ Discrimination	

Other relevant resources from Pavilion

A Mismatch of Salience: Explorations of the nature of autism from theory to practice

By Damian Milton

A Mismatch of Salience brings together a range of Damian Milton's writings that span more than a decade. The book explores the communication and understanding difficulties that can create barriers between people on the autism spectrum and neurotypical people. It celebrates diversity in communication styles and human experience by re framing the view that autistic people represent a 'disordered other' not as an impairment, but a two-way mismatch of salience. It also looks at how our current knowledge has been created by non-autistic people on the 'outside', looking in. *A Mismatch of Salience* attempts to redress this balance.

Available at: https://www.pavpub.com/a-mismatch-of-salience/

The Anger Box: Sensory turmoil and pain in autism

By Phoebe Caldwell

Shifting attention away from presentation and symptoms of autism alone, Phoebe explores and attempts to understand the sensory issues experienced by those on the autistic spectrum and their neurobiological roots in an effort to find new ways of alleviating the distress that can characterise people on the autistic spectrum.

Available at: https://www.pavpub.com/the-anger-box/

Hall of Mirrors - Shards of Clarity: Autism, neuroscience and finding a sense of self

By Phoebe Caldwell

Drawing on Phoebe Caldwell's 40 years of experience and expert knowledge of autism and Intensive Interaction, *Hall of Mirrors – Shards of Clarity* marries recent neuroscience research evidence and practical approaches used in care to cover a wide range of vital subjects. Sense of self, confirmation, sensory issues, case studies and neuroscience findings are explored and weaved together in an inspired way which brings aims to bring theory into practice and vice versa, while at the same time listening to the voices of people with autism. The result is to allow everyone in the autism field to take a few steps forward with how they interact and support autistic people.

Available at: https://www.pavpub.com/hall-of-mirrors/

Responsive Communication: Combining attention to sensory issues with using body language (intensive interaction) to interact with autistic adults and children

By Phoebe Caldwell, Elspeth Bradley, Janet Gurney, Jennifer Heath, Hope Lightowler, Kate Richardson and Jemma Swales

Responsive Communication is a groundbreaking book which has been put together by a team of authors led by Phoebe Caldwell, who during her long-time practice in this field has found some unique paths to achieving deep and meaningful engagement with autistic people and people with profound and multiple learning disabilities. The book explains how to communicate with children and adults who are struggling to understand and articulate speech using Responsive Communication. Responsive Communication combines Intensive Interaction (using people's body language to communicate) with attention to sensory issues, to encourage effective emotional engagement and reduce behavioural distress.

The authors offer a range of fascinating and informative perspectives on the approach and application of responsive communication, from backgrounds including expert by experience, communication, service management, occupational therapy, neuroscience and psychiatry. What this range of contributors has in common is a sense that before we can address communication, we need to attend to the sensory features of autism and reduce the information processing distress that may be hindering our ability to get in touch with our autistic partners.

Available at: https://www.pavpub.com/learning-disability/autism/responsive-communication

Understanding and Responding to Autism: The SPELL Framework (2nd edition)

by Julie Beadle-Brown and Richard Mills

A fully revised, new edition of *Understanding and Responding to Autism: The SPELL Framework (2nd edition)* including new video, self-study guide and learner workbook.

These new training and self-study resources reflect the changes in the autism context in the UK as well as in many other countries, and the valuable experience the authors have gained from many years of using the original resources for training in many different settings.

Available at: https://www.pavpub.com/learning-disability/autism/understanding-and-responding-autism-spell-framework-2nd-edition

10 Rules for Ensuring People with Learning Disabilities and those who are on the Autism Spectrum Develop 'Challenging Behaviour' … And maybe what we can do about it

By Damian Milton, Richard Mills and Simon Jones

Written in the voice of someone with autism, this pocket sized booklet directly addresses the many practices and assumptions that that cause so many problems for children and adults with autism and learning difficulties and their family, friends and carers.

Available at: https://www.pavpub.com/10-rules-for-challenging-behaviour/

Understanding Autism: A training pack for support staff and professionals based on 'Postcards from Aspie World'

By Dan Redfearn, Holly Turton, Helen Larder and Hayden Larder

This unique training pack is based on the premise that learning from the experience of someone on the autism spectrum can help those who support individuals to understand and to adapt their approach and therefore achieve better outcomes. Each pack comes with a set of postcards created by a young woman with Asperger's syndrome. The postcards are also available to buy separately and are a valuable resource to prompt and aid discussion.

Available at: https://www.pavpub.com/understanding-autism/

Choosing Autism Interventions: A research-based guide

By Bernard Fleming, Elisabeth Hurley and The Goth

This best-selling book provides an accessible evidence-based overview of the most commonly used interventions for children and adults on the autism spectrum. It summarises best clinical practice from the National Institute for Health and Care Excellence (NICE) and gives a set of tools to help you evaluate interventions for yourself. It is the first guide of its kind to meet the requirements of the NHS Information Standard.

Available at: https://www.pavpub.com/choosing-autism-interventions/

Autism Spectrum Conditions: A guide

by Eddie Chaplin, Steve Hardy and Lisa Underwood

Published in association with the Estia Centre, this guide provides a comprehensive introduction to working with people who have autism spectrum conditions.

Available at: https://www.pavpub.com/autism-spectrum-conditions/

Autism and Intellectual Disability in Adults Volume 1 & 2

Edited by Damian Milton & Nicola Martin

Autism and Intellectual Disability in Adults: Volumes 1 & 2 explore issues and practice affecting the support of adults with intellectual disabilities who are on the autism spectrum. This volumes explore potential key moments in the lives of adults with intellectual disabilities who are on the autism spectrum, covering a breadth of subjects including; policy, health, economics, wellbeing and equality, as well as a wealth of practical information and advocacy-related material. The focus of this series is not on the causes of autism; our interest instead lies in considering ways in which autistic people (focusing here on those with additional intellectual impairments) can have the best possible quality of life, on their own terms. Common themes emerge between authors, including the fundamental requirement to acknowledge, respect and facilitate autistic expertise as being central to the production of research, policy and practice.

Available at: https://www.pavpub.com/autism-and-intellectual-disability-in-adults-volume-1/ and https://www.pavpub.com/autism-and-intellectual-disability-volume-2/